Written by: Phil Yates, Wayne Turner
Editors: Peter Simunovich, John-Paul Brisigotti
Graphic Design: Casey Davies
Assistant Writers: Richard Chambers
Proof Readers: Andrew Haught, Mark Goddard, Sean Ireland, Mitch Kemmis, Paul Kitchin, Michael McSwiney, Huw Peregrine-Young, Stephen Smith, Greg Siter, Chris Townley

Miniatures Design: Evan Allen, Tim Adcock, Matt Bickley, Will Jaynes
Cover Art: Vincent Wai
Miniatures Painting: Aaron Mathie
Web Support: James Brown
Playtest Groups: Dad's Army (Gavin Van Rossum), Houston (Mike Callahan), La Brigada de Madrid (Jorge Sancho), Northern Battle Gamers (Nigel Slater).

CONTENTS

The Cold War	2
The Cold War Heats Up	6
Combat Team Yankee	8
Playing *World War III: Team Yankee*	14
How It Works	16
Teams and Units	18
Unit Cards	20
Terrain	24
Turn Sequence	28
Starting Step	29
Movement	**30**
Staying In Command	31
Moving Through Terrain	32
Transports and Passengers	34
Movement Orders	36
Shooting	**38**
Check Range	40
Check Line of Sight	40
Declare Targets	43
Rotate to Face	43
Roll to Hit	44
Assign Hits	45
Roll Saves	46
Destroyed Teams	49
Pinned Down	50
Firing Smoke	50

Artillery	**51**
Who Can Bombard	51
Pick Spotting Team	51
Check Range	51
Select Template Size	51
Select Aiming Point	52
Rotate to Face	53
Roll to Range In	53
Roll to Hit	53
Roll Saves	54
Pin Down Target	54
Repeating Bombardments	54
Special Artillery Ammunition	55
Smoke Bombardments	56
Assaults	**57**
Who Can Assault	57
Charge into Contact	57
Opponent's Defensive Fire	59
Roll to Hit	60
Roll Saves	61
Check if the Assault is Over	61
Test to Counterattack	62
Counterattack or Break Off	62
Consolidating	63
Unit Morale	**64**
Formation Morale	**65**
Weapon Special Rules	**66**
Equipment Special Rules	**68**
Special Abilities	**69**
Armies of the World	**70**
Force Structure	**76**

Picking Your Force	**78**
Missions	**82**
Selecting a Mission	82
Who Attacks	82
Deployment	83
Who has the First Turn	83
Winning the Game	83
Victory Points	83
Objectives	84
Mission Special Rules	85
Ambush	85
Meeting Engagements	86
Reserves	86
Strategic Withdrawl	86
Basic Missions	87
Annihilation	87
Free For All	87
Dust Up	88
Encounter	88
Counterattack	89
Hasty Attack	89
More Missions	90
Breakthrough	90
Rearguard	91
No Retreat	91
Bridgehead	92
Night Fighting	**92**
Minefields	**94**
Battle Plans	**95**
The *World War III: Team Yankee* Range	**96**
Index	**100**

All rights reserved. No part of this publication may be reproduced, stored in a retrieval system, or transmitted, in any form or by any means without the prior written permission of the publisher, nor be otherwise circulated in any form of binding or cover other than that in which it is published and without a similar condition being imposed on the subsequent purchaser.

© Copyright Battlefront Miniatures Ltd., 2019. ISBN: 9781988558127

THE COLD WAR

**Television news story
22 July:**

Despite condemnation by the UN, Western European nations, Japan, and the U.S., Iran has pledged to continue attacks on any vessel that enters the Persian Gulf, now declared a war zone by that country. Outside the Straits of Hormuz, entrance to the Persian Gulf, the number of tankers sitting at anchor, waiting for a break in the deadlock, continues to grow. The ships' owners and their captains feel that this deadlock will not last long. As one ship's captain stated, 'They have tried this before and always backed off. They need us too much to keep this up for long.'

**State Department press release
26 July:**

"The attack by Iranian war planes on commercial vessels in the international waters of the Indian Ocean yesterday is a threat to the security of the free world. The United States and the free world cannot allow such acts of deliberate terrorism to go unpunished. While the United States continues to pursue all available means to resolve this issue peacefully, military options are being considered.

**Department of Defense press release
27 July:**

The destroyer U.S.S. Charles Logan, while on patrol in international waters off the Straits of Hormuz, was rammed, then fired upon by a Soviet Cruiser of the Gorki class this morning. U.S. forces returned fire. Damage and casualties on either side are not known at this time."

**White House press release
28 July:**

In view of the current crisis, the President has issued an order federalizing 100,000 Army Reserve and National Guard personnel. Personnel and units affected have been notified and are reporting to their mobilization stations."

TASS news release, 28 July

A meeting of the Warsaw Pact ministers ended today with a pledge to stand together in the face of threats and increased war preparations on the part of the United States. Representatives from Poland, the German Democratic Republic, Hungary, Bulgaria, Czechoslovakia, and the Soviet Union released a joint statement pledging to meet American aggression against any member state with retaliation in kind.

Vatican press release, 29 July:

A request on the part of the Holy Father to travel to Moscow to talk to the Soviet premier in an attempt to find a peaceful solution to the current crisis was denied. The Holy Father calls for both sides to remember their responsibility to their people and to the world and again offered his services in any future negotiations."

BBC news release, 30 July:

"A stormy session between the French president and the Soviet foreign minister in Paris today ended when the Soviet foreign minister warned the French president that the national interests of France would best be served if that nation did not involve itself in the current crisis between the Soviet Union and the United States. In a statement immediately after the meeting, the president announced that France would stand by her treaties and do her part to defend Europe against aggression from any quarter. The president went on to announce that the French military forces, with the exception of its strategic nuclear forces, would actively cooperate with other NATO nations during the current crisis."

Television news story, 1 Aug:

"We interrupt this program for a special announcement. Unconfirmed reports from Brussels, headquarters for NATO, state that the NATO nations have ordered their armed forces to mobilize and commence deployment to wartime positions. While there is no official word from Washington concerning this, announcement of an address to the nation by the president at seven o'clock this morning, followed by a joint press conference by the secretaries of state and defense, seems to add credibility to these reports."

With the end of the Second World War in 1945, many hoped that peace might follow. These hopes were quickly dashed as the victors began squabbling over the spoils. For forty years, both sides faced each other across armed borders. Now, in 1985, this cold war is now a hot one. There is no more peace.

When the Germans took on the whole of Europe almost single-handedly in the Second World War, they sought to produce a bigger Germany. This would include much of Poland, Czechoslovakia, and some of France. When they lost the war, Germany not only lost all of their conquests, but Poland and the Soviet Union absorbed the eastern part of Germany.

Worse, the remaining part of Germany was split in four by the occupying Allied forces. Initially, this split was supposed to be a temporary administrative arrangement, but the formation of two opposing governments fixed this division in place. The Soviet-backed Communist government in the old capital of Berlin ruled the German Democratic Republic (GDR), known as East Germany, while the Western powers created a new government in Bonn to rule the remainder as the Federal Republic of Germany (FRG), known as West Germany. The city of Berlin mirrored this configuration, being divided in to four parts as well.

The divide between East and West intensified in 1949 when France, the United Kingdom, the United States, and other minor states formed NATO (North Atlantic Treaty Organisation), for mutual defence, and then intensified further when the Soviet Union responded with the creation of the Warsaw Pact, uniting all of the Soviet-aligned states, in 1955.

Defections to the West from Soviet countries led to the creation of the infamous Iron Curtain, a mined and wired border strip running from the Baltic Sea to the Balkans, and the Berlin Wall. These fortifications limited passage between the two blocs to a few, carefully-controlled checkpoints.

Insurrections in East Germany and Poland, along with revolutions in Hungary and Czechoslovakia that required full-scale invasions by the Soviet Army to quell, added to Soviet difficulties. While NATO did nothing to overtly assist the revolutionaries, these incidents increased tensions.

Initially, the threat of Mutually Assured Destruction (given the appropriate acronym, MAD) in a massive nuclear counterstrike limited the size of the standing armies on both sides of the Iron Curtain. However, by 1980, the new Multiple Independently-targetable Re-entry Vehicle (MIRV) missiles, capable of destroying a dozen targets at once, and Anti-Ballistic Missiles (ABM) had forced a more layered nuclear strategy.

Checkpoint Charlie, Berlin, 1961

THE COLD WAR

3

NATO AND WARSAW PACT DEPLOYMENT AND PLANNED WARSAW PACT ATTACKS

This change in strategy returned the emphasis to conventional warfare, and the 1970s saw a huge build up of military strength on both sides of the Iron Curtain, along with intensive efforts to modernise the ground forces' weaponry. Now in 1985, both NATO and the Warsaw Pact have huge armies deployed and ready to fight, with even more in reserve. The latest weapons are being deployed in ever-increasing numbers.

The main Soviet forces are the Group of Soviet Forces in Germany (GSFG) of 25 Soviet and German divisions in the GDR, the Northern Group of Forces (NGF) of 16 divisions in Poland, and the Central Group of Forces (CGF) of 15 divisions in Czechoslovakia, a total of 56 divisions with around 13,000 tanks. This doesn't count the divisions in the western parts of the Soviet Union that will form the immediate follow-on waves.

Facing these are LANDJUT (Land Forces Jutland) defending Denmark and the Baltic Approaches with 3 Danish and German divisions, NORTHAG (Northern Army Group) covering the North German Plain with 11 Belgian, British, German, and Netherlands divisions, CENTAG (Central Army Group) covering the Fulda Gap with 10 German and US divisions, and the French SOUTHAG (Southern Army Group) facing Czechoslovakia with six French and German divisions. Another 12 British, French, Netherlands, and US divisions are ready to reinforce them at the first sign of trouble. These 42 divisions muster about 9000 tanks.

KEY

Armoured Divisions — Each Symbol represents a Division. Armoured Divisions contain between 200 and 350 tanks and 11,000 and 20,000 troops

Mechanised Divisions — Mechanised Divisions contain between 50 and 220 tanks and 13,000 and 20,000 troops

NATO FORCES
- United States
- Great Britain
- West Germany
- Belgium & The Netherlands
- France

WARSAW PACT FORCES
- Soviet Union
- Czechoslovakia
- East Germany
- Poland

THE COLD WAR

COLD WAR HEATS UP

By 1985, the Soviet Union was in trouble. The hard-line Leonid Brezhnev had led the Soviet Union for eighteen years until his death in 1982. His successors were both old, sick men, and by April 1985, the post of General Secretary of the Central Committee was vacant again. Two decades of mismanagement and a war in Afghanistan (often described as the Soviet Union's Vietnam) had left the Soviet Union impoverished and discontented.

With a choice between the relatively young, reform-minded Mikhail Gorbachev and another hard-line Communist of the Stalin era, the Central Committee baulked*.

At this point, our story diverges from the history that followed Mikhail Gorbachev's appointment.

Reform could mean the end of the Soviet Union. Instead, they chose to hold on to their lives' works. A victorious war to seize the resources of Western Europe would distract the people from food shortages, and stripping the Capitalist's wealth would buy time for their economy.

The Committee's plan required three carefully-managed steps to guarantee success. The army's reserves would need to be called up and front-line divisions brought to full readiness without alerting the West to do the same.

Then, a surprise attack would need to capture Denmark and the Baltic Approaches to get the navy out into the Atlantic, keeping the United States' reserves trapped on the wrong side of the ocean. Finally, the army would need to reach the Rhine in a matter of days, taking the German industrial heartland and the ports of Netherlands before the West could fully react. With NATO's armies smashed and the Soviet army on the Rhine, the West would be forced to sue for peace, sacrificing Germany for their own safety.

A routine exercise, enlarged to a full-scale test of mobilisation procedures, gave the excuse to ready the army, while reassuring the West that nothing bad was planned. The Iran-Iraq War in the Persian Gulf provided the perfect setting for an incident that provided an excuse for further mobilisation to 'protect the Soviet Union from unprovoked aggression'.

Symbols on this map follow the same key as those on page 5, except that each symbol shows a Soviet Army or a NATO Corps rather than a Division

Loud protestations and vigorous diplomacy kept the West in a state of uncertainty, slowing their mobilisation. However, neither the US president, Ronald Reagan, nor the British Prime Minister, Maggie Thatcher, both strongly anti-Communist, delayed long in mobilising their forces. They quickly began the process of calling up reservists and preparing to send them to join their comrades in Europe. Other NATO countries followed suit, but mobilisation was still incomplete when the axe fell.

By Sunday, 4 August, 1985, everything was ready for the Soviet attack. Their forces crossed the border at dawn. By the end of the first day, Soviet operational manoeuvre groups had bypassed Hamburg and reached the ports of Kiel and Bremerhaven. The follow-on forces from the Northern Group of Forces were approaching the Danish border to meet up with naval forces landing on the coast. Third Shock Army was finding that its advance on Hannover across the North German Plain was progressing more slowly as the 1st British Corps slowly retreated on their main line of resistance. Further south, the American 5th Corps was holding the Fulda Gap through the mountains in strength, virtually halting the advance on Frankfurt in its tracks. The Central Group of Forces out of Czechoslovakia were making progress through the mountains of the Bohemian Forest on the border, and were making good progress through neutral Austria.

As the days passed, the northern thrusts were the only ones even remotely on schedule. The entire NORTHAG now pivoted on 1st British Corps and extended westward to the Dutch coast. From there the front line extended almost due south, with CENTAG holding the Soviet advance in the Fulda Gap well short of Frankfurt. In the south, the advance had bypassed Munich and almost reached Stuttgart.

With the entire French Army committed and the British Army sending the last of its Territorial Brigades into action, ready or not, the last NATO reserve were elements of the 3rd US Corps flown in from the United States to link up with pre-placed equipment. Things looked grim for NATO, but the Warsaw Pact was also running out of troops, having committed every available force to reach this far. Given time, both sides could muster more troops, but for the moment, that was everything.

It was at this point that NATO struck back with two major counterattacks. NORTHAG, using 3rd US Corps as a core, formed a multi-national force to strike from the British salient up towards Wilhelmshaven, aiming to cut off 2nd and 20th Guards Armies and the 1st Polish Army. Meanwhile CENTAG, having held the 1st Czechoslovak Army in front of Nürnberg, counterattacked reaching the Inner German Border with a thrust from 3rd German Corps. They then released part of 7th US Corps for a thrust towards Leipzig, and ultimately (if successful), Berlin. With these counterattacks, the war entered a new phase.

COMBAT TEAM YANKEE

The events in the background of *Team Yankee* are based on the novel by HW Coyle, then a soldier serving with the US Army in Europe. *Team Yankee* is about one company, or team, called Team Yankee, a tank-heavy combat team under the command of Captain Sean Bannon in West Germany. At the start of the story the Team consists of eighty four men and a mix of modern, high-tech weaponry as well as tried and true, if somewhat old, equipment. Although the Team is a tank-heavy company team, it is attached to 3rd Battalion, 78th Infantry (Mechanized), a mechanised infantry battalion.

TEAM YANKEE

Combat Team Yankee is a tank-heavy Formation under the command of a mechanised infantry battalion.

The Armored Combat Team has four Units, 2nd and 3rd Platoons equipped with M1 Abrams tanks, the Mech Platoon equipped with infantry-carrying M113 armoured personnel carriers, and an anti-armour platoon equipped with M901 ITV anti-tank missile tracks.

The M1 Abrams platoons each have four Tank Teams, all M1 Abrams tanks, plus two more in the HQ for a total of ten M1 Abrams and an M113 FIST (Fire Support Team). The Mech platoon has four Tank Teams (its M113 tracks) and seven Infantry Teams (the Unit Leader, three Dragon anti-tank Teams, and three rifle Teams) for a total of 21 soldiers. The attached anti-armour platoon has two M901 ITVs.

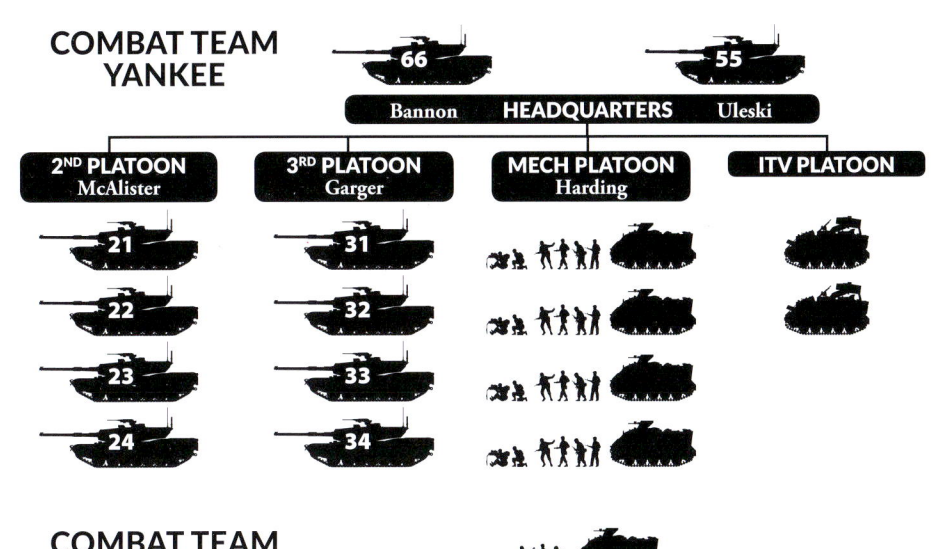

COMBAT TEAMS

The US Army cross-attached tank and mechanised infantry companies between battalions, giving each type some integral support from the other. These companies further cross-attached a platoon with one of their host battalion's companies, producing a combat team. Team Yankee is just such a combat team, having swapped its 1st platoon for a mech platoon from Bravo Company, forming Combat Team Bravo in the process.

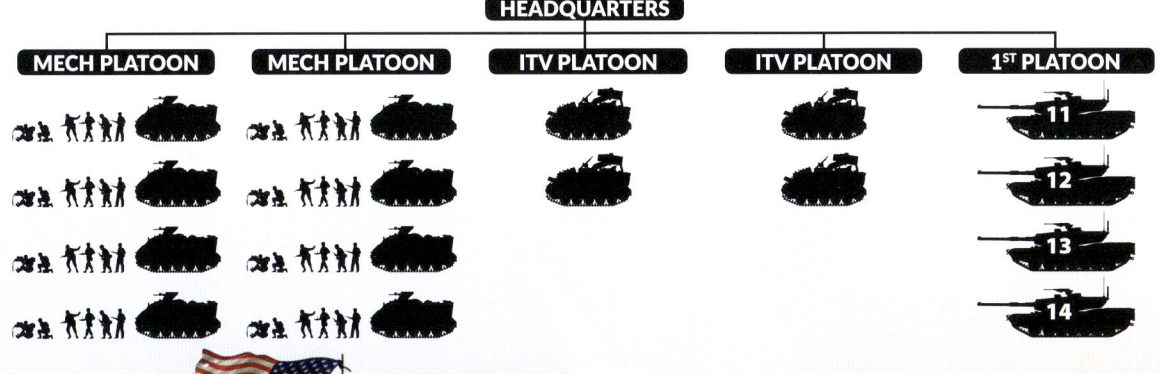

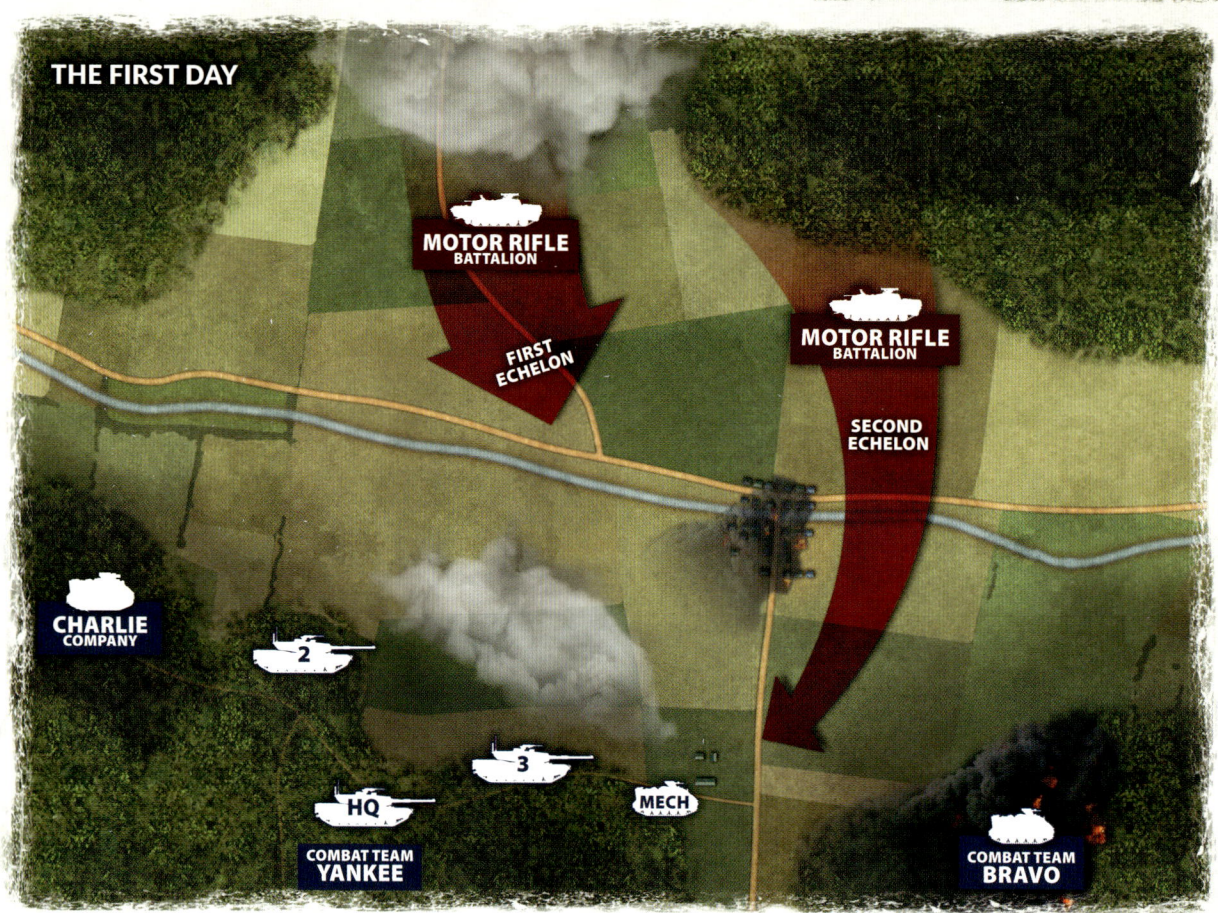

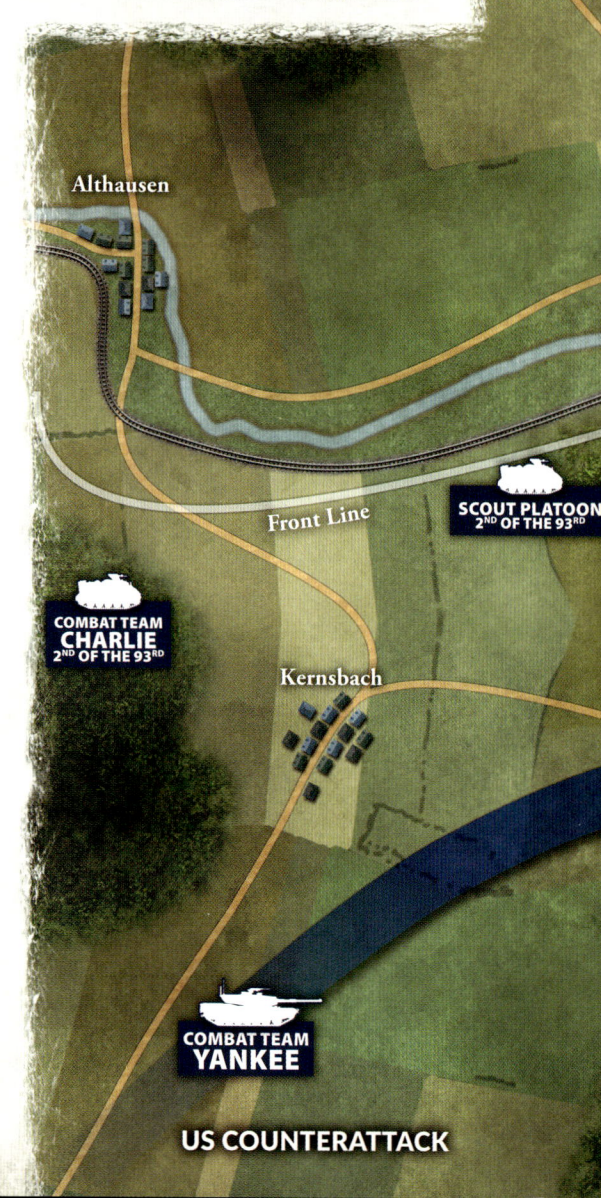

THE FIRST DAY
Mid-afternoon, Sunday 4 August

Team Yankee's war began as a battered cavalry screen withdrew through their position covering a river crossing at a village in the valley. An intense artillery strike heralded the arrival of the Soviet first echelon. Fortunately for Team Yankee, it landed on Team Bravo. Unfortunately, the artillery largely put Team Bravo out of the fight.

The first Soviet motor rifle battalion, weakened by its fight with the cavalry, pushed over the hill and down into the valley, heading diagonally across to the village. Team Yankee opened fire from the Soviet flank, destroying the battalion for little loss. The attack of the Soviet second echelon, also weakened by air and artillery fire, was preceded by a gas attack and covered by a smoke screen. Team Yankee's thermal sights and Lieutenant Garger's good tactics quickly eliminated this thrust as well.

US COUNTERATTACK
0600, Tuesday 6 August

1st Brigade had mauled the Soviet first echelon, but the Soviet 28th Guards Tank Division in the second echelon would soon take over the attack. Task Force 3rd of the 78th were relieved by the divisional cavalry and sent north to counterattack the flank of the Soviet division and disrupt their attack.

A night march in unfamiliar territory found Team Yankee and Team Bravo in position, but no sign of Charlie and Delta Companies that were supposed to support them. The irate Task Force commander ordered Team Yankee to attack anyway. All went well until Team Yankee, having negotiated the railway embankment, started to cross the stream. At that point the defenders of the small hill labelled Objective LOG opened fire. By the time Team Yankee had overrun the position in a wild charge, half of their vehicles were knocked out. Worse, Captain Bannon's radio was out, so his attempts to consolidate on the position, were in vain and his tanks raced on towards Hill 214, Objective LINK.

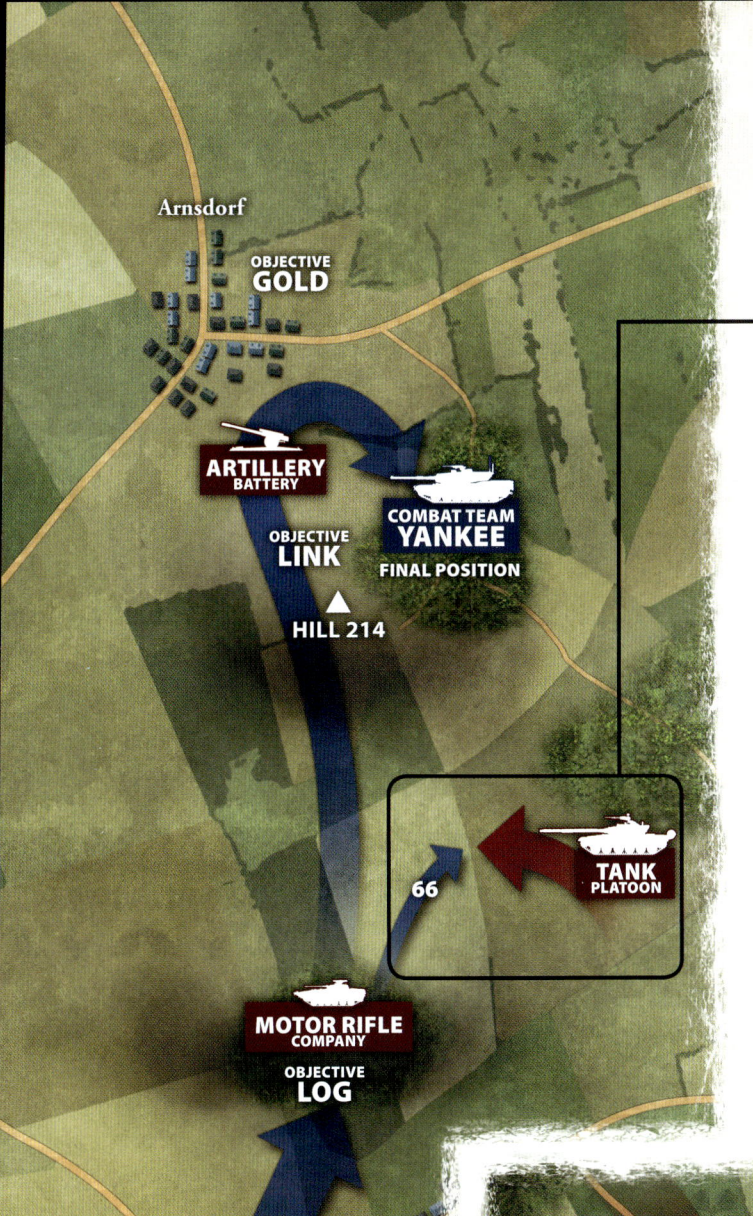

THE LAST BATTLE OF TANK 66
Mid-morning, Tuesday 6 August

Trying to catch up with the rest of his tanks, Bannon's tank '66' suddenly stopped, hung up on a tree stump. By the time they were mobile, the Team was long gone.

A platoon of Soviet T-62 tanks, aiming to hit the rest of Team Yankee in the rear, veered towards 66 as it exited the woods. Despite the Soviet tanks' first shot killing Ortelli, the driver, and setting the engine of 66 on fire, Bannon continued fighting, knocking out all three Soviet tanks, before finally abandoning 66.

THE BATTLE FOR HILL 214
Midnight, Wednesday 7 August

Having mopped up the last resistance on LOG, the two surviving M113 tracks of the Mech Platoon picked up Bannon's crew and joined the last four tanks on Hill 214. Under Uleski, the executive officer, the tanks had taken the hill, overrunning a Soviet artillery battery in the process.

After probing the American position, a Soviet motor rifle battalion that had re-occupied Arnsdorf launched a three-pronged attack on Hill 214 around midnight. Anticipating this possibility, Team Yankee had deployed to cover all three approaches, but with just one weak platoon in each direction. Despite this, better night-vision equipment and the sheer firepower of the M1 Abrams tank and M47 Dragon missile allowed the Team to repulse the attack. Exhausted, the entire Team was asleep when 1st Battalion, 4th Armor, Team Yankee's parent battalion, arrived to relieve them in the morning.

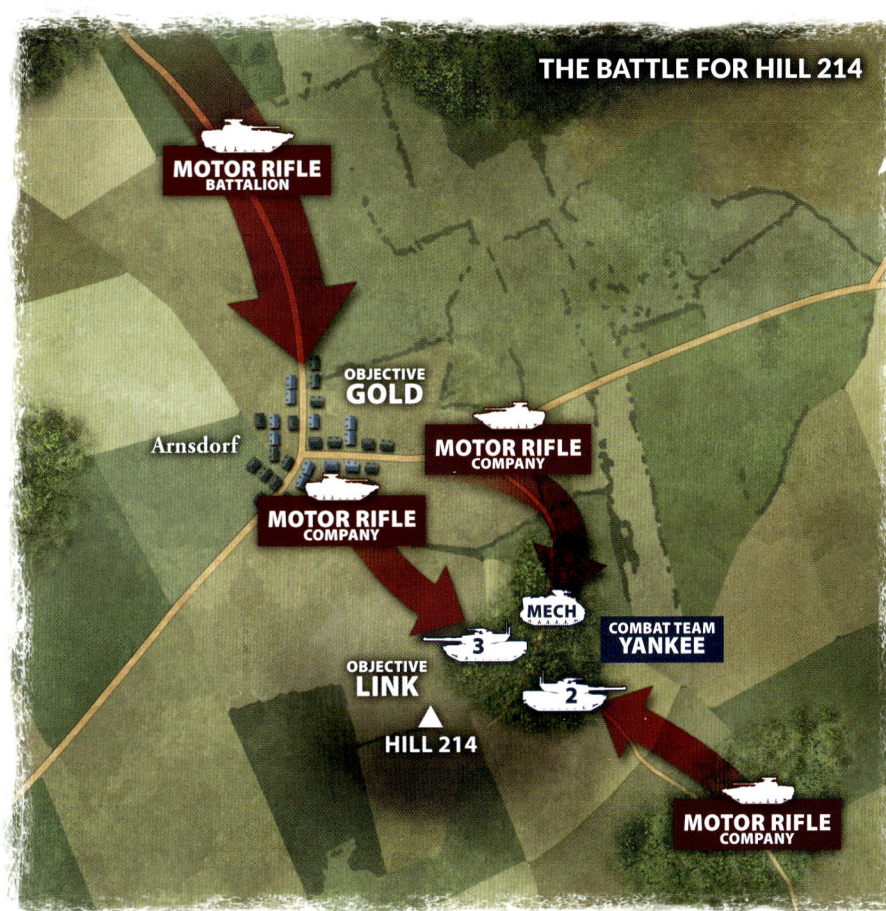

DEEP ATTACK
0400, Monday 12 August

After finding a gap between two Soviet armies, a German *Panzer* division launched an attack across the Inter-zonal Border into East Germany. Their thrust ran out of steam when it hit a Polish division.

Having spent several days recovering from its ordeal, Team Yankee was ordered to renew the attack. The initial objective was the town of Korberg, then on to the city of Leipzig, a major transport hub, and ultimately Berlin.

Fortunately for Team Yankee, the Polish division attacked the West German bridgehead just before Team Yankee attacked. Pummelled by the American artillery preparation, then mauled by the West Germans, the Poles were in no position to stop Team Yankee's breakthrough, but did manage to delay the rest of the Task Force that followed.

After waiting at Issel for the rest of the Task Force to catch up, Team Yankee was leading the way north again when a pair of Soviet Mi-24 Hind attack helicopters struck the Team's flank, knocking out an M1 Abrams tank in their first pass. The Hinds were surprised in turn, being driven off by a pair of AH-1 Cobra attack helicopters, leaving Team Yankee to advance again.

COUNTERATTACK
Morning, Monday 12 August

Team Yankee was approaching Korberg when Charlie Company's tracks started exploding. A Soviet T-72 tank company had counterattacked from a gap between two hills.

With the Task Force's command group knocked out, Bannon took control. While Delta Company turned to face the Soviet attack, Bannon ordered Team Bravo to swing south and attack the Soviet flank. Meanwhile, Team Yankee headed for the gap to cut off any following Soviet forces.

Reaching the gap and finding no more Soviet forces, Bannon sent the Mech Platoon into the woods to hold the flank, then launched his tanks into the retreating Soviets. Like medieval knights, the two tank forces charged through each other. When the smoke cleared the field was littered with burning T-72 tanks and another knocked out M1 Abrams.

FIGHT IN THE WOODS
Mid-morning, Monday 12 August

Lieutenant-colonel Potecknov, the Soviet battalion commander was having a bad day. His advanced guard had gone off the air, and his other two companies had been delayed by breakdowns. Then his lead element was ambushed. Under pressure from above to attack the American breakthrough immediately, he had no choice but to order his remaining tanks forward as fast as possible. Once they reached open ground, they would swing out into line abreast formation and attack.

Having knocked out the three-tank Soviet lead element in a close-range ambush, the Mech Platoon pulled back to the far side of the clearing and readied their Dragon missiles. There they were joined by Second Platoon's three M1 Abrams tanks.

Team Yankee had only just got into position when 18 T-72 tanks poured out of the woods. The odds weren't good, despite Team Yankee opening fire before the Soviet crews located them. All would have been lost had not a pair of A-10 Warthog aircraft intervened, smashing the last Soviet tank just 50m from Team Yankee's positions.

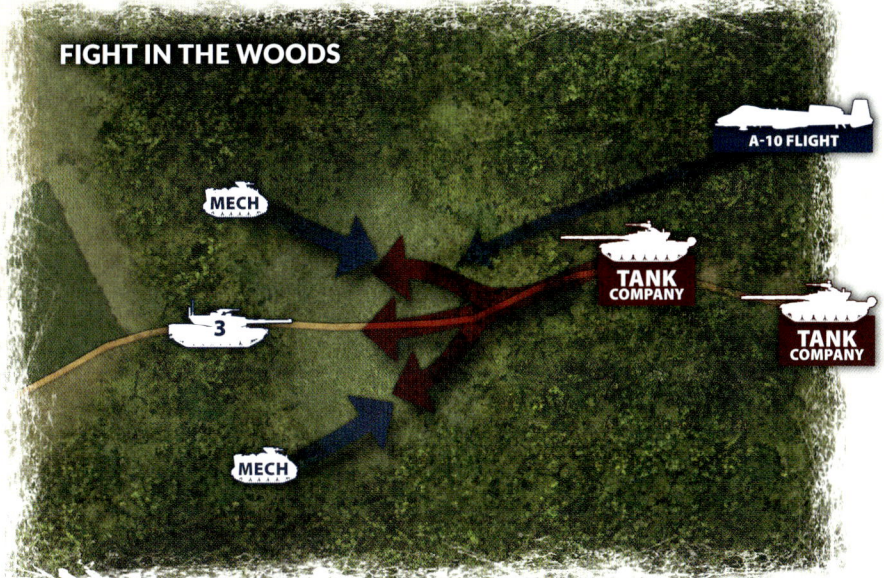

LANGEN GAP
Midnight, Monday 12 August

With the failure of the lead battalion's attack, the Soviet regimental commander switched his other two battalions to the Langen Gap, just east of Korberg. Task Force 3rd of the 78th was deployed to meet them. Delta Company, with the survivors of Charlie, were entrenched in Langen, covered by minefields.

When the Soviet tanks hit the minefields in the dark, Delta and Team Bravo opened fire. The disorganised Soviet tanks pushed on, bypassing Langen to the south. There they ran into another ambush as Team Yankee delivered the final blow. The few surviving T-72 tanks broke off and fled eastwards.

The victory was a hollow one for the Task Force. Its casualties put it out of the fight. After a few days rest, Team Yankee rejoined its parent battalion, the 1st of the 4th Armor, for the push to the Saale River and Leipzig beyond.

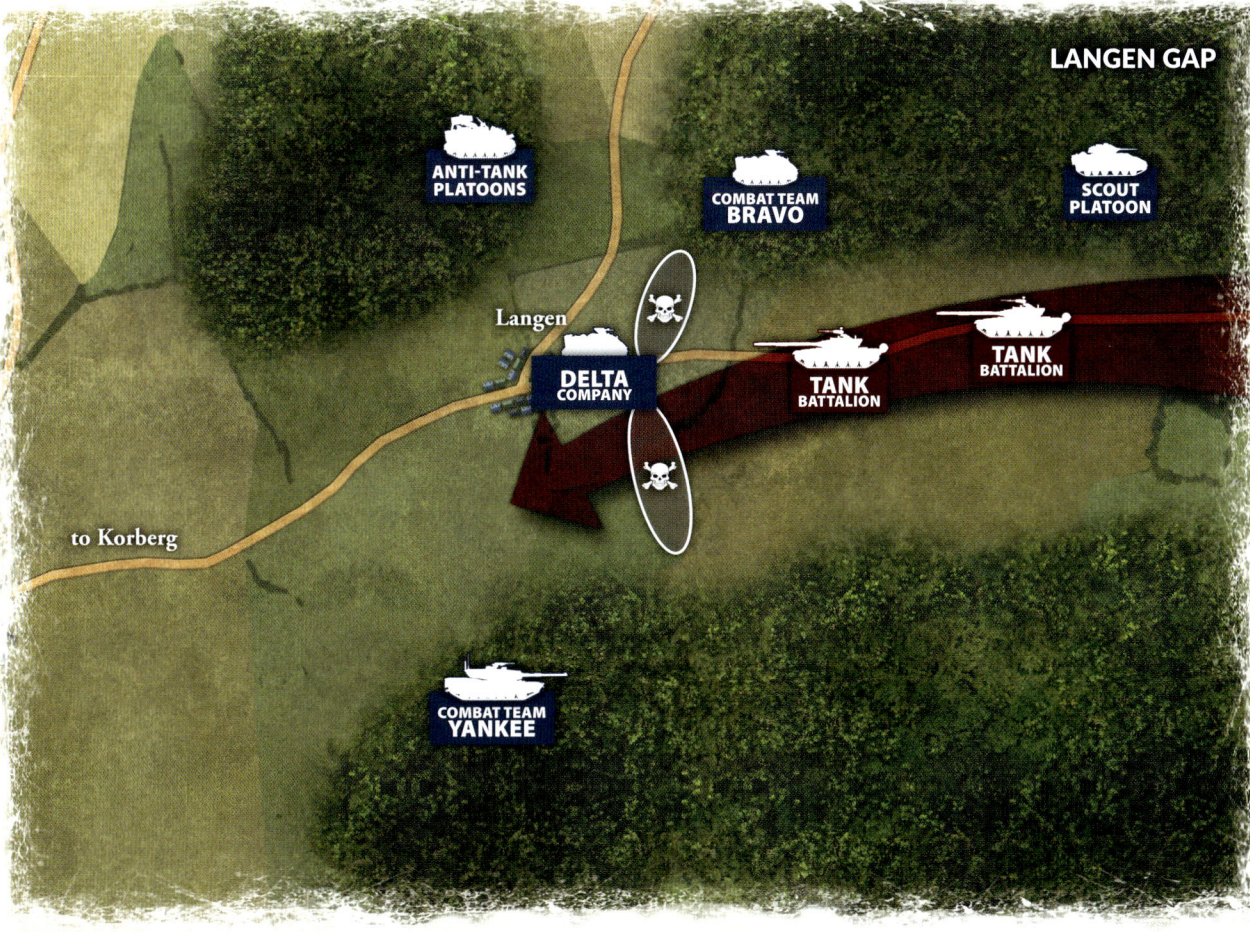

PLAYING TEAM YANKEE

The five T-72 tanks began their descent into the valley in a line with about 100 meters between tanks. One of them had a mine roller attached to the front of its hull. He would have to be taken out in the first volley. As soon as the tanks started down, a line of Soviet armored personnel carriers, BMP-2s, appeared on the crest of the hill and followed the tanks down without hesitation. There were fifteen of these personnel carriers deployed in a rough line about one hundred meters behind the tanks. All moved down the opposite slope at a steady and somewhat restrained pace, as if they really didn't want to go into the valley or get too far ahead of follow-on elements.

Captain Sean Bannon is facing his first battle and needs to decide what to do. Should he open fire immediately, hoping to knock out the first echelon before the follow-on elements arrive? Or should he wait until the entire Soviet force is in his kill zone, hoping that he still has the drop on them?

If you were Captain Bannon, what would you do? Would your plan work better than Sean's?

In *Team Yankee*, you get the chance to find out. You can set up a miniature battlefield with model tanks and soldiers representing the real-life troops that faced each other across the Iron Curtain in 1985. You and your opponent assume the roles of their commanders, pitting your wits and cunning against one another to attain victory and, more importantly, to have fun.

THE CHALLENGE OF COMMAND

Team Yankee allows you to re-fight the battles that might have been if the Cold War had gone hot. Would NATO have been able to hold against the immense power of the Soviet Union? Could the numerous Warsaw Pact tanks defeat smaller numbers of technically superior Western tanks? *Team Yankee* lets you find out.

This rulebook is your guide to fighting these battles in miniature. With it you can take command of a company or battalion of soldiers and pit yourself against cunning opponents on the field of battle. You will see for yourself whether the M1 Abrams really has what it takes to take on first-line Soviet equipment. You will find out if you have the guts to stop a massed charge, or the cold-blooded ruthlessness to launch one!

Team Yankee combines the joys of painting and modelling your own miniature army with the challenge of facing off against your opponent across a gaming table in a social setting, and you'll get to create history as it might have been!

GETTING STARTED

The easiest way of learning the rules is to visit a store or club where experienced players can run you through an introductory game and introduce you to other players.

If you don't have a store handy, you can teach yourself quite easily. Read through this book, don't worry about remembering it all, you can look it up again later, then play a small game with a friend.

The Last Battle of Tank 66 on the Team Yankee website, is a great place to start. Set up the four tanks, grab their Unit Cards, and start playing. Take it slowly at first, looking up the rules as you go, and by the end of the game you'll pretty much know how to play *Team Yankee*. Add a few more teams for the next game, and slowly build up your experience as you go. Before you know it, you'll be a veteran tank commander!

WEBSITE

The *Team Yankee* website is the ultimate resource for World War III gamers, whatever their level of experience. You'll find information about all the armies, unique downloadable content, inspirational photos, and all the latest news. The forum is the perfect place to meet other *Team Yankee* players and compare tactics, get advice on your next army, or find answers to all your rules questions. Go to *www.Team-Yankee.com* now!

WHAT YOU NEED

You don't need much to start a game of *Team Yankee*. Here's what you need.

AN OPPONENT
Team Yankee is a social game played by two or more players, so grab a friend and get started.

TWO ARMIES
The *Team Yankee* range of 15mm (1/100th) scale miniatures is specifically designed for the game and is available through all good hobby stores.

Each model comes with its own Unit Card showing its capabilities in the game.

THIS RULEBOOK
This rulebook contains all the rules you need to play *Team Yankee*.

A TEMPLATE
Artillery and aircraft are not precision weapons. Their shells and bombs blanket a wide area, possibly wiping out dozens of the enemy at a time. Artillery and Salvo Templates make it easy to work out who is hit, and who isn't when you introduce these weapons into your games (see page 52).

A BATTLEFIELD
Whether it's the kitchen table or a custom-built gaming table, you'll need a large flat surface to play the game.

A 6' x 4' (180cm x 120cm) board covered with a green sheet or painted and flocked makes an ideal battlefield.

TERRAIN
You'll need a selection of terrain like hills, woods, hedges, buildings, and roads to create a realistic battlefield for your troops to fight over.

The pre-painted terrain in the Battlefield in a Box range makes setting up a battlefield easy.

DICE
Team Yankee uses ordinary six-sided dice. You can personalise your force with army-specific dice marked with your force's insignia.

TOKENS
Even though they are toy soldiers, your troops react to heavy fire like real soldiers. Sometimes they get pinned down or bail out of their tanks. They get stuck in rough terrain and go to ground, hiding from the enemy. Tokens help you keep track of the state of your troops.

TAPE MEASURE
You'll need a tape measure or ruler to measure movement and shooting ranges. You can use Metric or Imperial measurements, whichever suits you best.

HOW IT WORKS

Reality is immensely complex and rather messy. This game has the advantage of giving players virtually unlimited opportunities to fight new battles and collect new armies. Unfortunately, it also requires rules to cover the many aspects of something as big as the battles of *Team Yankee*. The good news is that you don't need to know all of the rules to play the game. You can start with the basics and add things like artillery, aircraft, and even heli-borne assaults when you are ready.

To help you understand the rules, this section explains some of the concepts behind the game.

DIE ROLLS

Team Yankee uses the same standard six-sided dice that games like Monopoly and Yahtzee use.

When the rules say to roll a die, they give a number that you must equal or exceed, for example, 3+ (a roll of 3, 4, 5, or 6 means success), or 5+ (a roll of 5 or 6 means success). Any roll lower than the number means the attempt has failed.

In some cases, such as shooting at partially concealed targets, the number needed for success will be modified.

Add +1 to the required score for each of the modifiers that apply at the time. For instance, if you normally need a 3+ to hit the enemy, but the target was both (a) at long range and (b) concealed in a wood, the required score on each die would go up to 5+.

Sometimes the score required is shown as 'Auto'. This means that the roll will automatically succeed.

If the rules require you to roll more than one die, treat each roll as a separate success or failure.

RE-ROLLS

In some situations, where your first roll fails, you may be allowed a re-roll. A re-roll is just what the name says—you get to ignore the first attempt and roll the die again.

The score on the second die roll is what counts. You never get more than one re-roll per situation.

MEASURING

Team Yankee gives game measurements in both inches (Imperial) and centimetres (Metric). You should agree on which system you and your opponent will use before the game begins—you must use one of these two systems, not switch between both. Generally, it's a good idea to use the system you are most familiar with.

You are allowed to measure any distances on the battlefield any time you want to. You can measure how far your weapons can shoot, how far the opponent's weapons can shoot, or even whether or not you have enough movement to assault at the end of the turn. After all, your soldiers have maps, range-finders, and binoculars to help them work these things out.

TALK TO YOUR OPPONENT

You can make your game flow more easily by letting your opponent know what your intention is when moving your forces. If you tell them you are intending to stay out of range, or that you think your troops are completely out of sight behind a wood, it reduces disputes if a model gets bumped later.

WYSIWYG

Team Yankee is a What You See Is What You Get, or WYSIWYG, game. One miniature represents one soldier or vehicle. In many cases you can resolve difficulties by remembering this and taking a look at the situation from a model's-eye view, down on the ground so to speak. Have a look at what your miniature could see from where they are or where they could go on the terrain as modelled.

SPECIAL RULES

To keep things simple, the main part of the *Team Yankee* rules only cover the more common cases. Rules that are specific to certain weapons, vehicles, units, or armies are given as special rules.

These special rules either add additional capabilities or allow the teams and platoons that use them to break the normal rules. When a special rule conflicts with the normal rules, apply the special rule.

WHEN THINGS HAPPEN

Normally turns in *Team Yankee* follow a straightforward sequence. However, some rules, particularly special rules, cause things to happen out of turn. An example of this would be anti-aircraft weapons engaging enemy aircraft when they appear in the enemy turn.

When this happens, interrupt the normal turn sequence, resolve the unusual activity, then return to where you were and continue the turn.

WHEN THINGS GET TRICKY

In a hobby such as wargaming, it's impossible to over-emphasise the importance of being a good sport. Whether you are crushing your opponent or you are on the receiving end of an almighty pummelling, it's always good to remember that whatever the outcome of the battle, playing is all about having fun.

Some good basic rules are to be fair, play to the spirit of the game, treat your opponents with courtesy and respect, and don't get too bogged down with the rules. Oh, that and don't give up! The odds may look grim with your army set to be beaten, but hang in there. Some of the best stories are about heroic last stands and a few brave individuals turning the tide and holding out against the odds to finally snatch an unlikely victory.

Remember, whether you are facing a friend or a new opponent, treat them just the way you would like to be treated and you will get so much more from the hobby.

WORKING IT OUT

Sometimes it can be difficult to figure out how a rule should be applied to an unusual situation that has occurred in your game. If something unexpected happens, talk with the other players and try to come up with a good interpretation of what would happen. The best thing to do is to make a quick call that both you and your opponent can agree on.

If you can't come to an agreement quickly just roll a die:

- If you roll 4, 5, or 6, use your interpretation of the rule for the rest of the game.
- A roll of 1, 2, or 3, means that you have to accept your opponent's interpretation of the rule for the rest of the game.

After the game, when you have more time for discussion without holding up the battle, sit down and agree how you'll handle the situation in the future.

If you still aren't sure, you can always check out the forum at *www.Team-Yankee.com* and ask other players how they would handle the problem.

HINTS AND TIPS

There are hints and tips in various places to help you learn the game. These are not rules, just ideas on how to play the game quickly and simply.

TEAMS AND UNITS

The military knows that the strength of a well-coordinated group of soldiers is far greater than the sum of its parts. *Team Yankee* reflects this by organizing your force into Teams, Units, and Formations.

TEAMS

TEAMS
Although the acts of a few individuals are always glorified by the media back home, in reality a soldier never does anything on their own. Soldiers are trained to operate as a Team, and it is this teamwork that keeps them alive. In *Team Yankee* your miniature soldiers also operate in Teams. There are three main types of Teams: Tanks, Infantry, and Aircraft.

TANK TEAMS
Tank Teams include all manner of military vehicles, from the mighty M1 Abrams main battle tank, down to the lowly jeep. Tank Teams are either Armoured or Unarmoured. Some Tank Teams are also Transport Teams designed to carry infantry as passengers.

INFANTRY TEAMS
Infantry Teams include all troops fighting on foot. They can be equipped with Heavy Weapons like PKM light machine-guns, SA-14 Gremlin anti-aircraft missiles, and M47 Dragon anti-tank missiles.

AIRCRAFT TEAMS
Aircraft Teams include everything that flies, from Helicopters like the Mi-24 Hind gunship, to Strike Aircraft like the A-10 Warthog. Some, like the AH-1S Cobra, are Hunter-killers, sneaking around the battlefield before pouncing on the enemy.

UNITS

UNITS

Your Teams are grouped into Units, platoons for NATO forces and companies for Warsaw Pact forces, typically of three to ten tanks or 30 to 100 infantrymen. A Unit operates as one, manoeuvring across the battlefield together and engaging the same foes.

UNIT LEADERS

A Unit combines a group of Teams under the command of a Unit Leader: a NATO Lieutenant or a Warsaw Pact *Kapitan*. You may pick any Team in the Unit as the Unit Leader at the start of the game.

ATTACHMENTS

Attachments are additional Teams associated with a Unit. Infantry Units containing Transport Teams as a Tank Attachment (or vice versa) are split into two Units, an Infantry Unit and a Transport Unit (each with their own Unit Leader). Both parts of the Unit operate independently as separate Units, supporting each other, although they deploy as a single Unit.

INDEPENDENT UNITS

Small Units, such as an artillery observer, are Independent Units. These fight in support of larger Units. Independent Infantry Units often have a transport vehicle as part of their Unit, and unlike most transports, this remains as part of the Independent Unit. Independent units can use the Mistaken Target rule (see page 45) to reassign hits to nearby Units, but cannot Charge into Contact (page 57), nor take an Objective (page 76), and are ignored for Victory Points (page 75).

FORMATIONS

Units are gathered together into Formations, companies for NATO forces and battalions for Warsaw Pact forces. A Formation contains a number of combat Units, along with several Units of heavy weapons, scouts, and other troops to back them up.

While you must have at least one Formation in your Force, you can have as many as you like.

FORMATION COMMANDERS

Each Formation has an HQ Unit containing the Formation Commander: a NATO Captain or Major or a Warsaw Pact *Mayor* or *Podpolkovnik*, and their staff. The Commander is the Unit Leader of the HQ Unit and commands all of the Units in the Formation.

You may choose any non-Transport Team from the HQ Unit as their Commander at the start of the game. Unlike other Units, Transport Teams from the HQ Unit remain as part of the Commander's Unit.

COMMAND LEADERSHIP

A Commander's presence can inspire troops to fight harder. When a Unit's Leader is within 6"/15cm and in Line of Sight of their own Formation Commander (including Commander's own HQ Unit), the Unit may re-roll failed Counterattack, Rally, Remount, and Morale rolls.

As Support Units don't have their own Formation Commander, any Formation Commander may lead them, granting them re-rolls.

FORMATIONS

UNIT CARDS

Unit and Formation cards play a key role in Team Yankee. Select the cards corresponding to the various components of your force and use them for quick reference as you play the game. This section explains the layout of some typical cards and what the different ratings and information mean.

TANK UNITS

Combining speed, protection, and firepower, tanks are the core of any modern army. Tank units allow you to field tanks as part of your force.

UNIT NAME AND DESCRIPTION
This is the Unit's name and the main type of equipment it has.

NATIONAL SYMBOL
This symbol tells which country the card belongs to.

SPEED CHART
This shows how fast the Team can move Tactically while shooting, or while Dashing across Terrain, Cross-country in the open, or along a Road. *See pages 30 to 33.*

WEAPONS CHARACTERISTICS
This displays the performance of the weapons carried by the Team: how far they shoot, how many dice they roll, how well they penetrate armour and destroy targets, and any special rules. You may only use one type of weapon at a time, either the tank's main gun, or its machine-guns. *See pages 38 to 50.*

UNIT STRUCTURE AND POINTS
This gives you the structure of the Unit, showing how many Teams are in the Unit and the Points cost of the Unit. It also includes Points for understrength Units, and any options that the Unit has.

FRONT

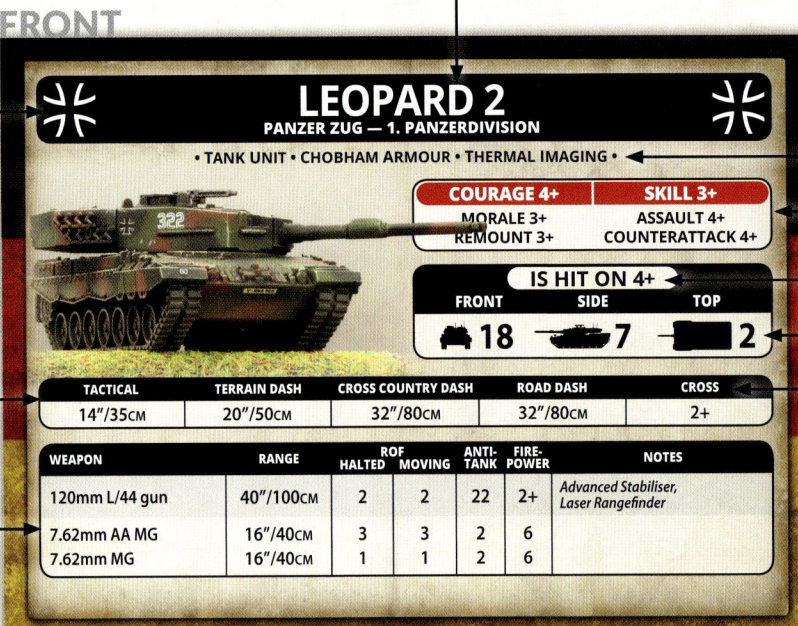

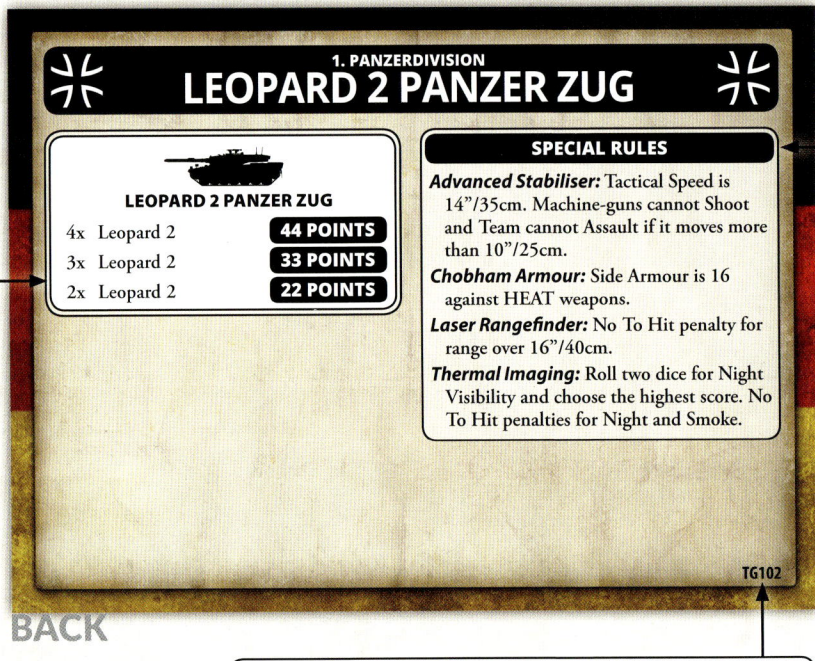

BACK

CARD ID
Each card is uniquely identified by its card ID, and are referenced by this number through-out this book.

MOTIVATION RATINGS

These show how likely the Unit is to pass a Courage test to do something brave, a Morale test to stay in the fight after heavy casualties *(page 64 and 65)*, a Counterattack test to counter-attack in an assault *(page 62)*, or a Remount test to get back in a vehicle after Bailing Out *(pages 47)*.

SKILL RATINGS

These show how likely the Unit is to pass a Skill test to do something difficult, or an Assault test to hit an enemy team in an assault *(page 60)*.

IS HIT ON NUMBER

This number tells you how easy it is for the opponent to hit this Team when shooting at it. *See pages 44 and 53.*

ARMOUR RATINGS

This shows how well protected an armoured vehicle like a tank is. *See page 46 and 47.*

Unarmoured Tank Teams have a single Save number instead. *See page 48.*

CROSS NUMBER

The Cross number shows how likely the Team is to cross Difficult Terrain without getting stuck. *See page 32.*

SPECIAL RULES

The Unit's special rules are listed here. The back of the card has a short summary of the rules. *See pages 66 to 69.*

ARTILLERY UNITS

While most tanks are designed to tackle the enemy head on, artillery sits back at a distance shelling the enemy from long range.

ARTILLERY WEAPON

An Artillery weapon has the word 'ARTILLERY' or 'SALVO' instead of a number for its ROF. *See pages 51 to 54.*

DIRECT FIRE

Most artillery weapons can shoot like a tank, directly at their target, rather than firing an artillery bombardment. Use this line instead when you do this.

SPECIAL AMMUNITION

Some artillery have specialist ammunition like bomblets, minelets, or guided projectiles, giving you more options when they come to shoot. *See page 55.*

INFANTRY UNITS

Infantry form an essential counterpart to your tanks. They are resilient and ideal for taking or holding villages and woods. Infantry cards are essentially the same as Tank cards, with a few changes shown on this page.

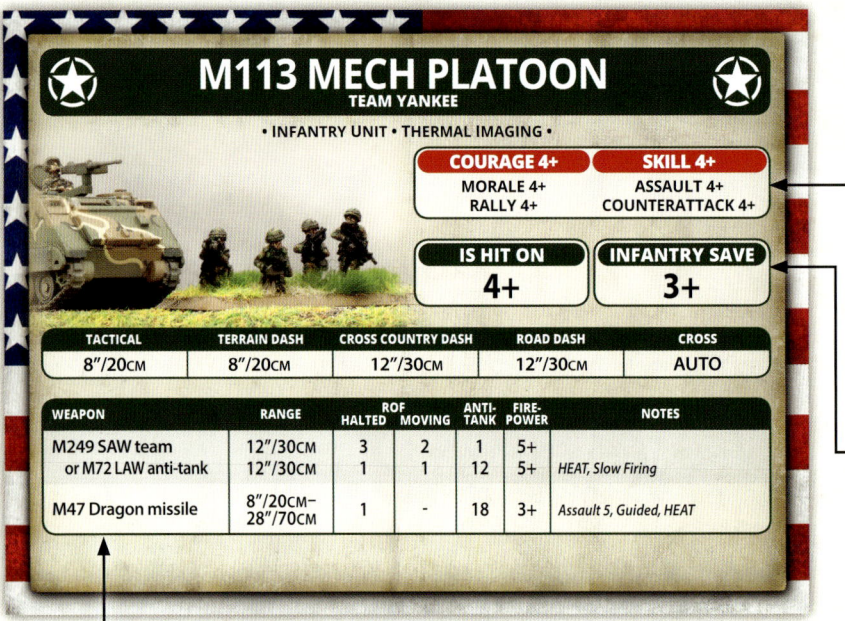

RALLY NUMBER
The Courage and Skill box is the same for Tanks and Infantry, except rather than Remount, Infantry have a Rally number showing how likely they are to recover from being Pinned Down. *See page 50.*

INFANTRY SAVE
This shows the number that a Team from the Unit needs to survive a hit. *See page 48.*

WEAPONS CHARACTERISTICS
Infantry Unit cards show all of the weapons used by the Unit. Most teams have a single line, although some versatile teams like the AK-74 assault rifle team have a secondary weapon that they can use instead, in this case RPG-18 anti-tank rockets. *See page 38.*

TRANSPORT UNITS
Although purchased as part of an Infantry Unit, the transports operate as a separate Tank Unit.

These are shown on separate cards. For the M113 Mech Platoon, their M113 armoured personnel carriers have their own Tank Attachment card showing their attributes. *See pages 19 and 34.*

TRANSPORT UNITS

ATTACHMENTS
Attachments like the M113 Transports of a M113 Mech Platoon have their own Unit card. Rather than describing the structure of the Unit, the card refers you back to its parent Unit card.

TEAM YANKEE — M113 TRANSPORT

M113 TRANSPORT
Transport Attachment to Team Yankee M113 Mech Platoon [TU104]

Dragon Mount: M47 Dragon missile teams may fire while mounted as M47

SPECIAL RULES
Amphibious: Treat Impassable Water as Difficult Terrain.
Guided: No To Hit penalty for range over 16"/40cm. Cannot hit Infantry unless they are stationary in Bulletproof Cover.
HEAT: Target Armour is not increased for range over 16"/40cm. Affected by BDD, Bazooka Skirts, Chobham, and ERA armour.
Passengers: Team can carry three Infantry Teams as Passengers.
Thermal Imaging: Roll two dice for Night Visibility and choose the highest score. No To Hit penalties for Night and Smoke.

TU105

M113 TRANSPORT — TEAM YANKEE
• TANK ATTACHMENT • AMPHIBIOUS • DRAGON MOUNT • PASSENGERS 3 • THERMAL IMAGING •

COURAGE 4+	SKILL 4+
MORALE 4+	ASSAULT 5+
REMOUNT 4+	COUNTERATTACK 5+

IS HIT ON 4+
FRONT	SIDE	TOP
3	2	1

TACTICAL	TERRAIN DASH	CROSS COUNTRY DASH	ROAD DASH	CROSS
10"/25CM	16"/40CM	24"/60CM	32"/80CM	3+

WEAPON	RANGE	ROF HALTED	ROF MOVING	ANTI-TANK	FIRE-POWER	NOTES
.50 cal AA MG	20"/50CM	3	2	4	5+	
Optional M47 Dragon missile	8"/20CM–28"/70CM	1	-	18	3+	Guided, HEAT

AIRCRAFT UNITS

Helicopters and strike aircraft give you the ability to project firepower anywhere on the battlefield. Aircraft cards are essentially the same as Tank cards, with a few changes shown below.

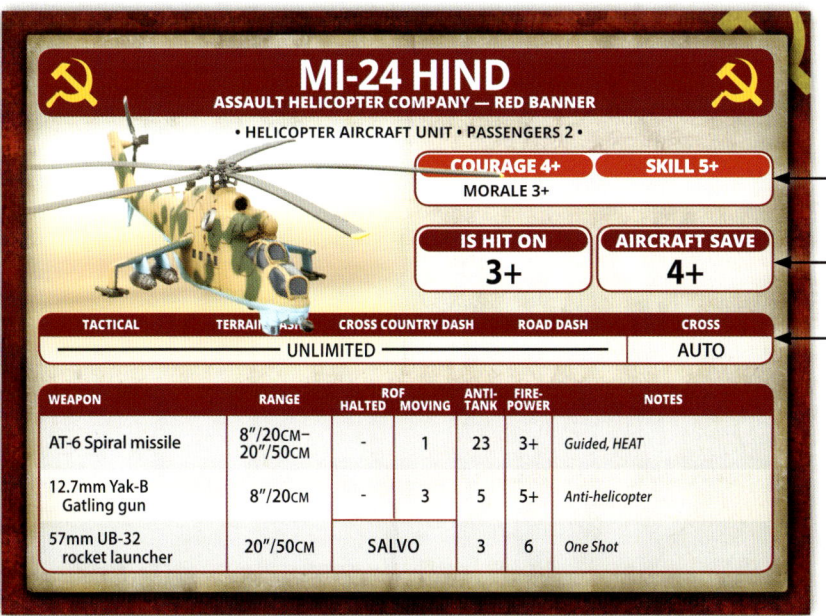

MI-24 HIND — ASSAULT HELICOPTER COMPANY — RED BANNER
• HELICOPTER AIRCRAFT UNIT • PASSENGERS 2 •

COURAGE 4+	SKILL 5+
MORALE 3+	

IS HIT ON	AIRCRAFT SAVE
3+	4+

TACTICAL	TERRAIN DASH	CROSS COUNTRY DASH	ROAD DASH	CROSS
UNLIMITED				AUTO

WEAPON	RANGE	ROF HALTED	ROF MOVING	ANTI-TANK	FIRE-POWER	NOTES
AT-6 Spiral missile	8"/20CM–20"/50CM	-	1	23	3+	Guided, HEAT
12.7mm Yak-B Gatling gun	8"/20CM	-	3	5	5+	Anti-helicopter
57mm UB-32 rocket launcher	20"/50CM	SALVO		3	6	One Shot

ABOVE THE MUD
Aircraft fly above the battlefield, taking no part in Assaults and cannot be Pinned Down. As a result, they have fewer ratings.

AIRCRAFT SAVE
This shows the number that a Team from the Unit needs to survive a hit. *See page 48.*

UNLIMITED SPEED
Aircraft fly so fast that they can move anywhere on the table. *See page 30.*

STRIKE AIRCRAFT
Some Aircraft Units do not remain on the battlefield. Instead these Strike Aircraft appear, make an attack, then leave the table. *See page 29.*

TERRAIN

Bannon faced front and eyed the next obstacle, a stream that, like the railroad embankment, ran perpendicular to their direction of travel. The first PC was already down in the stream and halfway across when he caught sight of it. The stream itself was not very wide. Centuries of erosion, however, had created a ditch some twenty meters in width with embankments a meter high. Upon reaching it, Ortelli eased 66 down into the stream bed, crossed with ease, and began to climb the far bank. They were halfway up it when the shit hit the fan.

Woods, hedges, bogs, bridges, rivers, lakes, rocks, rubble, and buildings all break up the terrain and complicate the battlefield. Sometimes this will be to your advantage, since your troops (whether riflemen, tanks, gunners, or trucks) can hide themselves among the clutter and put something solid between them and any bullets flying around. Other times these features will be a hindrance, as they impede your movement, slowing your advance to a crawl.

ROADS
Roads allow tanks to move much faster on them than they would cross-country.

There are five types of ground conditions that units can encounter:

ROADS
Whether concrete, brick, cobble, or dirt, a road provides a quick route from one place to another. Teams moving on roads travel faster.

CROSS COUNTRY
The majority of the table is usually easily crossed, although at a slower speed than on a road. Unless otherwise stated the parts of the board that are not covered by Terrain are rated as Cross Country terrain.

TERRAIN
Terrain features severely limit the speed at which vehicles can move. It ranges from ground that has been churned to mud to natural obstructions like woods.

WALLS
Walls are Difficult Terrain, requiring care to cross to avoid getting stuck and halting movement.
Walls are Short terrain, Concealing teams behind them. Stone and concrete walls provide Bulletproof Cover for teams immediately behind them.

DIFFICULT TERRAIN
Difficult Terrain is Terrain that presents a significant hindrance to movement. Vehicles attempting to move through this terrain risk getting stuck if the driver isn't careful.

CRATERS
Craters are Difficult Terrain, making them risky for tanks to cross.
Craters are Short terrain giving Bulletproof Cover to Infantry sheltering in them.

GENTLE HILLS
Gentle hills are Terrain, but don't present any risk of tanks getting stuck. Hills are Tall terrain, so block line of sight. Teams half hidden by a hill are Concealed and in Bulletproof Cover.

ROUGH HILLS
Steep hills are Difficult Terrain. Tanks are likely to have difficulty crossing them.

TREE LINES
Tree Lines are Difficult Terrain, requiring caution from tanks attempting to cross them. Tree lines are Tall terrain, so block line of sight. Teams immediately behind a tree line are Concealed.

RAILWAY LINES
Railway lines are Terrain, slowing troops as they cross them. They are Flat, so offer no concealment.

BUILDINGS
Buildings are Terrain that is Impassable to tanks. Infantry can enter and exit them through openings like doors and windows.
Buildings are Tall terrain. You cannot see past a building, although teams half-hidden by or in a building are Concealed. Buildings give troops inside Bulletproof Cover.

DISCUSS TERRAIN WITH YOUR OPPONENT
Everybody sees terrain slightly differently, so it is a good idea to discuss the terrain with your opponent before the game. Most of the terrain on your battlefield will be fairly obvious, but its better to sort out questions like is that hill gentle or steep, or is that river shallow or deep, at the beginning of the game rather than discover that you and your opponent have different views when you attempt to drive across it!

OPEN SPACES
Most battlefields are Cross-country apart from specific terrain features. Stationary infantry are Concealed in the open (and other Flat terrain), but tanks and moving infantry are in full view.

IMPASSABLE
Some obstacles, such as deep rivers, foetid swamps, or sheer cliffs, are just so difficult that it's impossible to cross them. Impassable obstacles stop all movement, forcing you to look for an alternative route to the objective.

HEIGHT OF TERRAIN

As well as helping or hindering movement, terrain also provides concealment and cover for troops on the battlefield. Terrain comes in three heights: Flat, Short, and Tall.

FLAT TERRAIN
Flat terrain, like roads, rivers, and ploughed fields, offer neither concealment nor cover to troops.

SHORT TERRAIN
Short terrain, like walls, hedges, crop fields and low rises, Conceal teams within or beyond them and may provide Bulletproof Cover (depending on what the terrain is).

TALL TERRAIN
Tall terrain like woods and buildings blocks line of sight, hiding whatever is behinds them. Troops on the edge can be seen, but are Concealed.

PLOUGHED FIELDS
Ploughed Fields are Terrain as they are difficult to move across at speed.

VINEYARDS AND ORCHARDS
Vineyards and orchards are Difficult Terrain. Tanks need to exercise care to avoid getting stuck.
Vineyards and orchards are Tall terrain like woods.

BUILDINGS
Man-made structures like buildings are different from natural terrain. They are solid, so troops can't be seen on the other side, but troops can enter them and fight through their openings, such as doors and windows.

Multi-storey buildings have one or more rooms on each level, making them, in effect, two buildings stacked upon each other.

Buildings more than about 6"/15cm across should be divided into rooms between 3"/7.5cm and 6"/15cm across. Treat each room as a separate building with openings into each adjacent room.

WOODS
Woods are Difficult Terrain. Tanks moving through a wood must make a Cross Check.
Woods are Tall terrain. Teams at the edge of a wood are Concealed.

FENCES AND HEDGES
Fences are Terrain, limiting the speed at which they can be crossed. Hedges are Difficult Terrain, requiring care when crossing to avoid getting stuck.
Fences and Hedges are Short terrain, Concealing teams behind them.

BROOKS
Brooks are Terrain, slowing tanks down as they cross.

LAKES AND PONDS
Lakes and Ponds are Impassable.
Water features are Flat terrain, so do not provide Concealment.

CROP FIELDS

Standing crops are Terrain. Tanks moving through them need to slow down to avoid hidden obstacles and potential infantry ambushes.
Standing crops Short terrain, Concealing teams in and behind them.

WOODS

Woods are impractical if they are modelled realistically in a WYSIWYG fashion. It would be difficult to place models in them or move them around inside.

Instead, this type of Terrain is modelled as a base to show the limits of the terrain and what is inside and what is outside of it, with trees placed on top to indicate the type and height of the terrain. The trees can be moved around on the base to allow your teams to move within the area of terrain, but are always assumed to be uniformly distributed throughout the area.

RIVERS AND FORDS

Shallow rivers are Difficult Terrain, slowing tanks and causing them make a Cross Check.
Deep rivers are Impassable to tanks, and require a 4+ Cross Check for infantry to cross. Teams cannot end their movement in a river or lake. Fords across deep rivers are Difficult Terrain.

River crossings are often the site of battles as rivers are significant obstacles. Think about why the battle is being fought here. Is the river a defence line? Has the attacker already taken a bridgehead across the river, and this is a counterattack to eliminate the bridgehead? Place the river and crossings accordingly. It's a good idea to have at least three ford or bridges unless you are planning to have infantry make an assault crossing.

WHAT YOU SEE IS WHAT YOU GET (WYSIWYG)

Most terrain features are represented quite literally on the table top. A house represents a house, exactly as it is shown. A hill represents a hill, exactly as shown. A wall represents a wall, exactly as shown.

This makes it easy to work out the answer to questions like 'Can my tank see over that wall?' by looking at the actual terrain feature placed on the table. Is the wall taller than your tank? If so, then it will probably have a great deal of difficulty seeing over it! Is the wall taller than the height of the gun barrel? If so, the tank will not be able to shoot over it. If its lower than that, the tank should have no problems seeing and shooting over the wall.

One exception to the WYSIWYG principle is bases on terrain. A lot of area terrain is based (usually on a base ⅛"/3mm thick) for manufacturing reasons. This raises terrain like roads and fields above the surrounding terrain, but should be ignored during play.

TURN SEQUENCE

Once more Bannon's mind wandered off the matter at hand. Several hours ago, somewhere in the division's rear, while Team Yankee was still knee-deep in Russians the division's commanding general had turned to his staff and pointed at a spot on the map. "Attack there." While the first sergeant and Sergeant Folk had been dragging the bodies of Team Yankee's dead to an out-of-the-way spot, the brigade commander had told the battalion commander, "Attack there." Now the executor of the plan, the lead element commander, the lowest ranking person in the U.S. Army to carry the coveted title of Commander, had his marching orders.

You are in command. Your job is to make that attack. In *Team Yankee*, players take turns at moving, shooting, and assaulting with all of their units. Once you have finished your turn, your opponent moves, shoots, and assaults with their units.

Each turn is broken into four steps: **Starting Step**, **Movement Step**, **Shooting Step**, and the **Assault Step**.

YOUR TURN

THE STARTING STEP (PAGE 29)

In the Starting Step, you step back from the battle and check how your soldiers are handling the stress of combat, how close you are to winning, and attempt to bring forward more troops.

THE MOVEMENT STEP (PAGE 30)

In the Movement Step, you manoeuvre your troops into position to shoot or assault the enemy (or to avoid the enemy doing the same to you!).

THE SHOOTING STEP (PAGE 38)

After completing the Movement Step, your troops open fire on the enemy in the Shooting Step. During the Shooting Step you shoot or fire an artillery bombardment with any or all of your Units, one at a time.

THE ASSAULT STEP (PAGE 57)

Once the Shooting Step is completed, your troops charge the enemy in the Assault Step, attacking them with hand grenades, close-combat weapons, and rifle butts, up close and personal.

YOUR OPPONENTS TURN

STARTING STEP

THE STARTING STEP

In the Starting Step, you check and update the status of units under your command, rally your troops, and organise fire support and reinforcements for your embattled soldiers. During the Starting Step you:

1. Remount Bailed Out Tanks *(see page 47)*
2. Rally Pinned Down Units *(see page 50)*
3. Check Unit Morale *(see page 64)*
4. Check Formation Morale *(see page 65)*
5. Reveal Ambushes *(see page 77)*
6. Roll for Reserves *(see page 78)*
7. Roll for Strike Aircraft *(see page 29)*
8. Remove Friendly Smoke Markers *(see pages 50 and 56)*

ROLL FOR STRIKE AIRCRAFT

STRIKE AIRCRAFT

The air force has many tasks across the breadth and depth of the battlefield. Your battle is just one small part of the big picture to them, so the aircraft supporting you will often be called away to more urgent tasks.

STRIKE AIRCRAFT ARRIVE

At the start of each of their turns, the owning player may roll a die. On a score of 4+, the Strike Aircraft Unit arrives and will be placed anywhere on table in the Movement Step as long as the Aircraft stand can be placed flat on the table or suitable terrain.

Aircraft shoot or bombard as normal in the Shooting Step. Just before an Aircraft attacks, the enemy can shoot their Anti-aircraft weapons at it (see page 39).

STRIKE AIRCRAFT DEPART

All Strike Aircraft are removed from the table at the end of the Shooting Step. Any casualties they suffer carry over when the Unit returns to the table.

STRIKE AIRCRAFT IN RESERVE

If the Strike Aircraft Unit is held in Reserve (see page 78), do not start rolling until the Unit arrives from Reserve.

HELICOPTERS

Unlike Strike Aircraft, Helicopters remain on the table from turn to turn operating like flying tanks. Helicopters are sufficiently fast that they can Move anywhere on the table. Simply place them where you want it in each Movement Step.

LOITERING OFF TABLE

Helicopters can leave the table instead of moving. The helicopter flies off to a safe location nearby, awaiting a call to return and engage new targets. It can return in a future Movement Step by moving back on to the table.

A Loitering Helicopter may not use a Movement Order to move on to the table, but may use them once it has moved onto the table.

MOVEMENT

The Poles were reeling from the bloody nose the Germans had given them. This was the ideal time to strike, while they were still confused. "Now is the time to speed up, not slow down."

The colonel agreed, ordering him to go for it. When Bannon dropped to the Team net and ordered Garger to pick up speed, hit hard, and keep rolling, all he got back from 3rd Platoon was a simple "I heard that."

MOVEMENT SEQUENCE

In the Movement Step you can move any or all of your Units. When a Unit moves, move each of its Teams up to its Movement rating. A Team can Move less than its maximum Movement if you wish, and a Team that does not Move will often be more effective at shooting.

TACTICAL AND DASH SPEEDS

There are two basic types of movement: Tactical and Dash. Tactical movement is used while engaging the enemy, while Dash movement is a high-speed dash to close the range or get into cover, but prevents the Team from shooting that turn.

AIRCRAFT MOVEMENT

Aircraft are sufficiently fast that they can Move anywhere on the table. Simply place the aircraft where you want it in each Movement Step.

GOING TO GROUND

Teams that do not Move, Shoot, or Assault are Gone to Ground, making them harder for the enemy to shoot at if they are also Concealed.

Gone To Ground token

MOVING

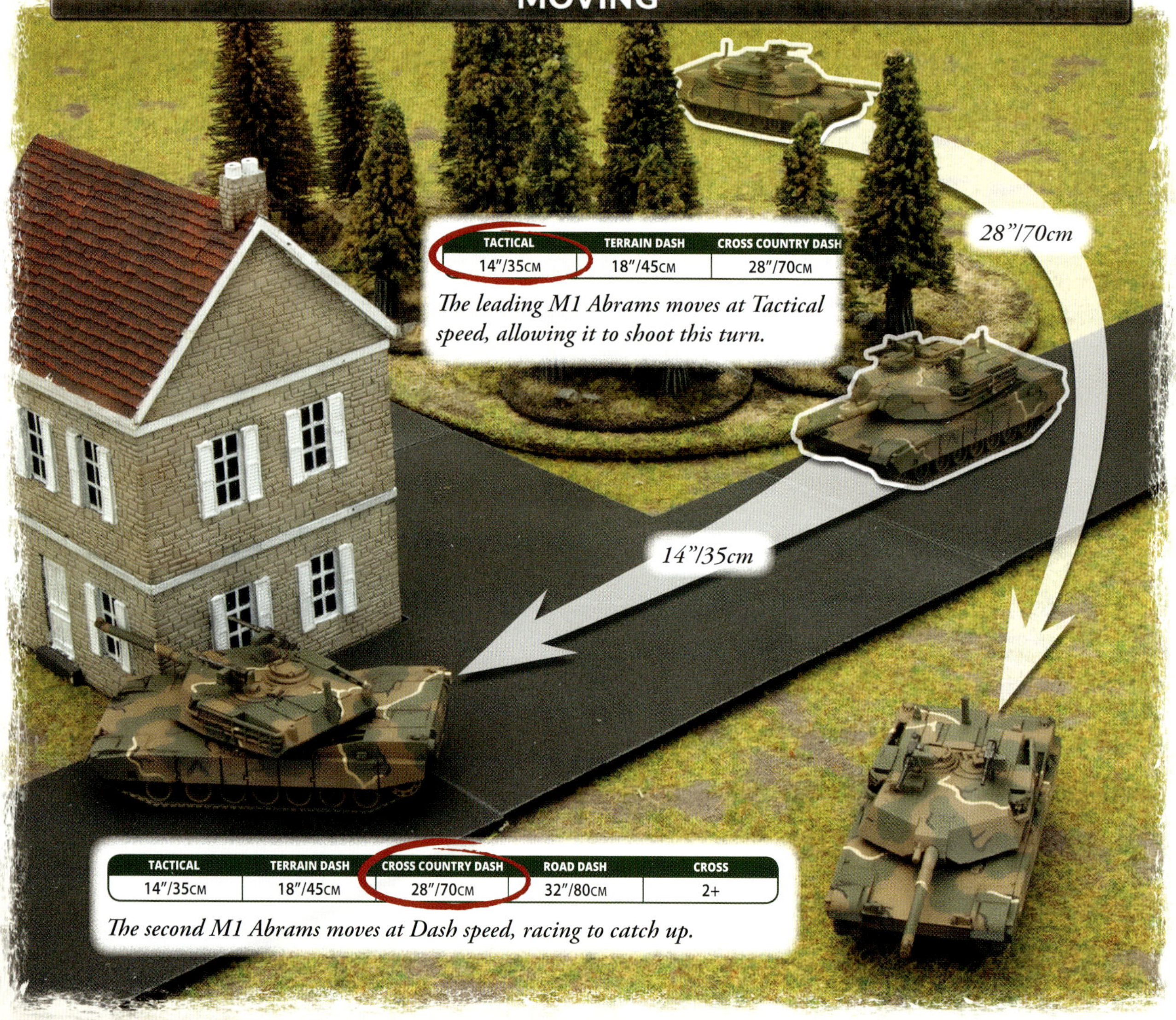

TACTICAL	TERRAIN DASH	CROSS COUNTRY DASH
14"/35CM	18"/45CM	28"/70CM

The leading M1 Abrams moves at Tactical speed, allowing it to shoot this turn.

28"/70cm

14"/35cm

TACTICAL	TERRAIN DASH	CROSS COUNTRY DASH	ROAD DASH	CROSS
14"/35CM	18"/45CM	28"/70CM	32"/80CM	2+

The second M1 Abrams moves at Dash speed, racing to catch up.

IN COMMAND

This T-72 ended its movement not within 6"/15cm of the Unit Leader, so is Out of Command.

This T-72 also ended its movement within 6"/15cm of the Unit Leader, so is also In Command.

Unit Leader

This T-72 ended its movement within 6"/15cm of the Unit Leader, so is In Command.

STAYING IN COMMAND

A Team that is In Command can Move, Shoot, and Assault normally.

- Any Aircraft Team, or any Team from a Unit with at least eight Teams is In Command if it ends its Move within 8"/20cm of its Unit Leader.
- A Team from a smaller Unit is In Command if it ends its Move within 6"/15cm of its Unit Leader.

A Team that does neither of these is Out of Command.

OUT OF COMMAND

A Team that will not end its Movement In Command (one that is Out of Command) must:

- remain in place with no penalty, or
- Move at Tactical speed, suffering a penalty of +1 to the score it needs to hit, or
- Move at Dash speed directly towards its Unit Leader, avoiding intervening obstacles.

MOVING THROUGH TEAMS

Tank and Infantry Teams cannot Move at Dash speed within 8"/20cm of any enemy Tank or Infantry Team.

Infantry Teams cannot move within 2"/5cm of any visible enemy Tank or Infantry Team in the Movement Step.

Tank Teams cannot move within 2"/5cm of any visible enemy Infantry Team, in the Movement Step.

Tank Teams cannot move through other Tank Teams under any circumstances.

OUT OF COMMAND

The Unit Leader has raced off, leaving the rest of their company Out of Command, and with limited movement options.

Unit Leader

The tanks can: Dash directly towards the Unit Leader, …

…Or remain in place to shoot with no penalty, …

…Or make a Tactical move, suffering a +1 penalty on its shooting.

MOVING THROUGH TERRAIN

This T-72 does not fit between the building and the woods.

…Or go around it at Tactical or Cross-country Dash speed.

It can either go through the woods at Tactical or Terrain Dash speed, taking a Cross Check, …

MOVING THROUGH GAPS

A Team can move through any gap it will fit through (ignoring its base if it has one). If the gap is too small to pass through, the Team will have to move through the surrounding terrain.

MOVING THROUGH TERRAIN

A Team's Tactical movement speed is not affected by the terrain it is moving over. The Team is focussing on taking cover, so is moving slowly anyway.

A Team's Dash movement speed depends on the type of terrain it is crossing: Road, Cross-country, or Terrain. If a Team spends its whole Dash move on a Road, it can move rapidly at Road Dash speed. If it spends any of its Dash move in Terrain, it moves at its Terrain Dash speed. Otherwise, it moves at its Cross-country Dash speed.

DIFFICULT TERRAIN

Some terrain is also difficult to cross. Each time a Team attempts to enter or starts moving in Difficult Terrain, the player must roll a die

- If the score is greater than or equal to the Team's Cross number, it successfully crosses that piece of terrain.
- Otherwise, the Team stops moving immediately. Even if the team is still where it started, it has now moved.

If a Unit Leader fails a Cross Test, you may nominate another Team from the Unit within 6"/15cm as the new Unit Leader to allow the Unit to continue moving.

IMPASSABLE TERRAIN

Some terrain is Impassable to some or all types of Teams. This terrain cannot be entered or crossed by those Teams.

CROSS CHECK

A pair of M113 APCs attempt to enter some woods, so they have to pass a Cross Check.

On a roll of 4, the first M113 will enter the woods without incident.

	TERRAIN DASH	CROSS COUNTRY DASH	ROAD DASH	CROSS
CM	16"/40CM	24"/60CM	32"/80CM	3+

On a roll of 2, the second M113 gets stuck as it tries to enter the woods and just immediately stop moving.

TERRAIN	DASH SPEED	CROSS CHECK	HEIGHT	BULLETPROOF COVER
OPEN SPACES				
Grass or Steppe	Cross-country Dash	No	Flat	No
Firm Sand or Thin Snow	Cross-country Dash	No	Flat	No
Soft Sand, Snow, or Mud	Terrain Dash	No	Flat	No
VEGETATION				
Ploughed Field	Terrain Dash	No	Flat	No
Crop Field or Open Scrub	Terrain Dash	No	Short	No
Orchard or Vineyard	Terrain Dash	Yes	Tall	No
Woods and Forests	Terrain Dash	Yes	Tall	No
HEDGES AND WALLS				
Fence	Terrain Dash	No	Short	No
Hedge	Terrain Dash	Yes	Short	No
Bocage Hedge	Terrain Dash	Yes	Tall	Yes
Line of Trees	Terrain Dash	Yes	Tall	No
Stone Wall	Terrain Dash	Yes	Short	Yes
HILLS				
Low Rise	Cross-country Dash	No	Short	Yes
Gentle Hill	Terrain Dash	No	Tall	Yes
Steep or Rocky Hill	Terrain Dash	Yes	Tall	Yes
BANKS, GULLIES, & CLIFFS				
Gully Access or Floor	Terrain Dash	No	Flat	No
Gully Side	Terrain Dash	Yes	Tall	Yes
Steep Bank or Low Seawall	Terrain Dash	Yes	Short	Yes
Cliff, Cutting, or High Seawall	Impassable	Impassable	Tall	Yes
WATER				
Brook	Terrain Dash	No	Flat	No
Creek or Shallow River	Terrain Dash	Yes	Flat	No
Ford across a Creek or River	Terrain Dash	Yes	Flat	No
Deep River	Terrain Dash for Infantry Impassable to Tanks	4+ Cross Check	Flat	No
Soft Ground	Terrain Dash	Yes	Flat	No
Swamp or Lake	Impassable	Impassable	Flat	No
ROADS AND RAILWAY LINES				
Road or Airfield	Road Dash	No	Flat	No
Track	Cross-country Dash	No	Flat	No
City Streets	Terrain Dash	No	Flat	No
Railway Line	Terrain Dash	No	Flat	No
Low Embankment	Terrain Dash	Yes	Short	Yes
High Embankment	Impassable	Impassable	Tall	Yes
BUILDINGS				
Doors and Windows	Terrain Dash for Infantry Impassable to Tanks	No	Short	Yes
Exterior Walls	Impassable	Impassable	Tall	Yes
Inside Buildings	Terrain Dash	No	Short	Yes
Rubble or Craters	Terrain Dash	Yes	Short	Yes
WRECKS				
Wrecked Tanks & Aircraft	Terrain Dash	No	Short	Yes

Since the M113 hasn't moved yet, it can now make a Dash move.

The Mech Platoon moves into its M113 tracks to mount up.

TRANSPORTS AND PASSENGERS

Transport vehicles can carry infantry, giving them protection from enemy fire and getting them across the battlefield faster.

PASSENGERS IN TRANSPORTS

Some Tank Teams (known as Transport Teams), including infantry fighting vehicles and personnel carriers, can carry passengers. The Passengers special rule has a number after it indicating how many Infantry Teams the Team can carry. While being carried as passengers, a Team cannot Shoot or Assault.

PASSENGERS ON TANKS

Up to three Infantry Teams can ride on the top of any Armoured Tank Team as Passengers, although they are more vulnerable to enemy fire (see page 35).

MOUNTING TRANSPORTS

An Infantry Team can Mount a Transport Team from their Transport Unit by Moving to it in the Movement Step.

If the Transport Team has not yet Moved, it can then Move at Dash speed (it cannot Shoot or Assault). Once mounted, a Team cannot Shoot or Assault.

DISMOUNTING FROM TRANSPORTS

An Infantry Team can Dismount from a Transport Team by Moving from its passenger compartment in the Movement Step before the Transport Team Moves.

A Team cannot Mount and Dismount in the same turn.

TRANSPORT AIRCRAFT MUST LAND

A Transport Aircraft must Land in order to Mount or Dismount passengers. It can only Land at the end of its Move, so must Land in the turn before it intends to pick up or drop off Passengers. The Transport takes off again when it next Moves.

Arriving at the town, the Mech Platoon moves out of its M113 tracks to dismount.

Once the passengers have dismounted, the M113 moves onto the flank to cover them.

TRANSPORT AIRCRAFT

The Mi-24 Hind helicopter ends its move by landing at an intersection deep behind enemy lines. Because it has already moved, the infantry of the Assault Landing Company cannot dismount yet.

In their turn, the enemy shoots at the helicopters.

Next turn, the infantry dismount and the helicopter takes off to strafe the enemy.

A Transport Aircraft may not land within 4"/10cm of an enemy team, and may not Shoot while Landed. If an enemy Team Moves within 4"/10cm of a Landed Aircraft, it immediately takes off, remaining in the same place as a Flying Aircraft.

SEND TRANSPORTS TO THE REAR
You must remove all empty unarmed Transport teams from the table at the end of any Step, and may remove any other empty Transport teams at the same time.

Transport teams removed in this fashion do not count as Destroyed, and if Bailed Out (see page XX), automatically Remount.

BRING TRANSPORTS FORWARD
Before moving a Unit, you may place all of its Transport teams (other than those that have been Destroyed) that have been Sent to the Rear or did not deploy on the table, back on the table.

The Transport teams must be placed within 4"/10cm of a Team from their Unit, and may not be:
- within 16"/40cm of any enemy Team within Line of Sight, unless Concealed by Terrain from it, or
- within 4"/10cm of any enemy Team.

Once Brought Forward in this way, the Transport Teams must move at Dash Speed (and therefore cannot shoot or assault this turn), but may Mount Passengers before moving.

SHOOTING AT PASSENGERS
While Mounted in or on a Tank Team, Passengers cannot be targeted.

PASSENGERS IN TRANSPORTS
If a Transport Tank Team or Landed Aircraft is Destroyed by Shooting or an Artillery Bombardment, roll an Infantry Save for each Passenger Team. Place the surviving Infantry Teams as close as possible to the Destroyed Transport on the side away from the Team that Destroyed it, facing in any direction. The surviving Teams of the Unit are automatically Pinned Down (*See page 50*).

If a Transport Team is Destroyed multiple times by an enemy Unit's shooting, each Passenger Team still only rolls one Infantry Save to see if they survive.

If a Transport Team is Destroyed in an Assault, all of its Passengers are also Destroyed.

Passengers in a Transport Aircraft that is not Landed are Destroyed when their Transport is Destroyed.

PASSENGERS ON TANKS
Each time a Tank Team is hit by Shooting or an Artillery Bombardment or in an Assault, any Passengers riding on top of it are automatically hit as well. Teams hit in this way are not in Bulletproof Cover (the tank attracts too much fire from all angles to protect the infantry) and take Infantry Saves (*See page 48*) and can be Pinned Down (*See page 50*) as normal.

BLITZ MOVE

SKILL 5+
ASSAULT 5+
COUNTERATTACK 4+

The Unit Leader issues a Blitz Move Order, trying to sneak the infantry up to the edge of the woods. They roll a Skill Test.

On a roll of 5+, the infantry can sneak 4"/10cm forward, not counting as having moved.

Otherwise, the whole Unit is Out of Command. It can still move forward using its normal movement, but being Out of Command, suffers an additional +1 penalty to its shooting.

MOVEMENT ORDERS

A Unit Leader may issue one Movement Order each turn. These allow their Unit to use clever tactics, cross terrain, dash ahead, or dig in.

BLITZ MOVE — SKILL

The Unit Leader can issue a Blitz Move Order in the Movement Step before its Unit Moves. If it does this, roll a die:

- If the score is greater than or equal to their Skill rating, the Unit Leader and any Teams that are In Command may immediately Move up to 4"/10cm before making a normal Tactical Move.

  If a Team Moves using Blitz Move, but does not Move any further, it is not considered to have Moved and can Shoot at its Halted ROF.

- Otherwise, Teams from the Unit can only Move at Tactical speed and automatically suffer the +1 To Hit penalty as if they had Moved Out of Command (see page 31).

FOLLOW ME — COURAGE

In the Movement Step after their Unit has finished moving, a Unit Leader can issue a Follow Me Order. If it does this, the Unit Leader Moves directly forward up to an additional 4"/10cm and rolls a die:

- If the score is greater than or equal to the Unit Leader's Courage rating, Teams in its Unit that are In Command may immediately Move directly forward up to an additional 4"/10cm remaining in Command.
- Otherwise, the rest of the Unit remains where it is.

Whether they succeed or not, all Teams from the Unit that are In Command cannot Shoot this turn.

FOXHOLES

Foxholes token

FOLLOW ME

COURAGE 4+
MORALE 3+
RALLY 3+

The Unit Leader issues a Follow Me! Order to get into cover and immediately moves another 4"/10cm forward. They roll a Courage Test.

On a roll of 4+, the T-72's within 6"/15cm move forward as well. On any other roll, the rest of the Unit remains where it is.

Either way, none of the T72's within 6"/15cm of the Unit Leader can shoot.

SHOOT AND SCOOT

An M1 Abrams ambushes the enemy. To avoid return fire, the Unit Leader issues a Shoot and Scoot Order to try to duck back through the woods. They roll a Skill Test.

Passing the Skill Test, the M1 can move 4"/10cm instead of assaulting (taking a Cross Check for the Difficult Terrain).

Otherwise, it stays right where it is and face the enemy's return fire.

SHOOT AND SCOOT — SKILL

A Unit Leader that did not move in the Movement Step can issue a Shoot and Scoot Order in the Assault Step instead of Assaulting. If it does this roll a die:

- If the score is greater than or equal to the Unit Leader's Skill rating, the Leader and any Teams that are In Command and that did not Move in the Movement Step may immediately Move up to 4"/10cm.
- Otherwise, the Unit remains where it is.

CROSS HERE

The Unit Leader can issue a Cross Here Order in the Movement Step before its Unit Moves. If it does this, any Teams (including the Unit Leader) from the Unit rolling to Cross Difficult Terrain within 6"/15cm of where the Unit Leader crosses improve their chance of crossing safely, reducing their Cross Test by 1. Teams using this order cannot Shoot or Assault this turn.

DIG IN — SKILL

The Unit Leader can issue a Dig In Order instead of Moving in the Movement Step. If it does this, any of the Unit's Infantry Teams may attempt to dig Foxholes instead of Moving. Roll a die:

- If the score is greater than or equal to the Unit's Skill rating, mark the selected Infantry Teams as being in Foxholes.
- Otherwise, the Unit failed to dig in.

Whether or not they succeeded in digging Foxholes, the selected Teams cannot Move, but Shoot with their Moving ROF, and cannot fire an Artillery Bombardment this turn. If they do not Shoot or Assault, they are Gone to Ground.

Once they have dug Foxholes, Infantry Teams have Bulletproof Cover (see page 48) and are Concealed (see page 42) until they Move.

CROSS HERE

Not wanting to take chances with his tracks getting stuck and stopping, the Mech Platoon's M113 Unit Leader issues a Cross Here Order.

Unit Leader

Any tracks from the platoon that cross within 6"/15cm of the Unit Leader pass their Cross Check on a 2+ instead of a 3+.

SHOOTING

Bannon intended to hold fire until the Soviet lead elements reached the valley floor. When that happened, the Team would engage them with both tank platoons and the ITVs simultaneously. The 2nd Platoon would engage the lead element, the 3rd Platoon would hit the enemy still on the opposite slope, and the ITVs would engage supporting vehicles such as BRDM-2s armed with anti-tank guided missiles on the far hill.

"ROMEO 25, THIS IS MIKE 77. SPOT REPORT. 5 T-72 TANKS MOVING WEST. GRID 190852. CONTINUING TO OBSERVE, OVER."

Bannon snapped his head to the left. There was no need to use a map. There was only one place where the Russians would be, and that was on the hill 2,200 meters away.

SHOOTING SEQUENCE

In the Shooting Step, you shoot with any or all of your Units one by one. When a Unit shoots, each Team that wants to shoot in the Unit picks an enemy Team as its target and shoots its weapons. Once you've finished shooting with one of your Units, move on to the next until all of the Units that you want to shoot with have shot.

1. Check Range *(see page 40)*
2. Check Line of Sight *(see page 40)*
3. Check for Concealment *(see page 41)*
4. Declare Targets *(see page 43)*
5. Rotate to Face *(see page 43)*
6. Roll to Hit *(see page 44)*
7. Assign Hits *(see page 45)*
8. Roll Saves *(see page 46)*

WHICH WEAPONS CAN FIRE

A Tank or Aircraft Team may either fire:
- all of its Machine-guns (MG), or
- one other weapon.

An Infantry Team may only fire one of its weapons.

SHOOTING AT TANKS & INFANTRY

You can shoot at Tank and Infantry Teams with any weapon in the Shooting Step.

SHOOTING AT AIRCRAFT

Flying Strike Aircraft can only be shot at by:
- Anti-aircraft weapons (Dedicated AA, Guided AA, or weapons whoses name includes 'AA MG').

WEAPON CHARACTERISTICS

Each weapon in a Unit has a line in its card describing its performance and effectiveness.

WEAPONS — This lists all of the weapons in the unit

RATE OF FIRE (ROF) — The maximum number of shots the weapon can take in one turn. Each weapon has a Halted ROF and a Moving ROF.

NOTES — Special abilities or rules of the weapon.

WEAPON	RANGE	ROF HALTED	ROF MOVING	ANTI-TANK	FIRE-POWER	NOTES
AK-74 assault rifle team	8"/20CM	3	3	1	5+	*Pinned ROF 1*
or RPG-18 anti-tank	8"/20CM	1	1	14	5+	*HEAT, Slow Firing*
RPG-7 anti-tank team	12"/30CM	1	1	17	4+	*Assault 6, HEAT, Slow Firing*
PKM LMG team	16"/40CM	7	4	2	6	*Assault 6, Heavy Weapon*
SA-14 Gremlin AA missile team	48"/120CM	3	-	-	5+	*Assault 6, Guided AA, Heavy Weapon*

RANGE — The maximum distance the weapon can shoot.

ANTI-TANK — The armour penetration of the weapon.

FIREPOWER — The ability of the weapon to destroy a tank after penetrating its armour or to knock out a dug-in position.

38

SHOOTING AT TANKS, INFANTRY, AND LANDED AIRCRAFT

Any weapons can be used to shoot at Tanks, Infantry, and Landed Aircraft.

Tanks and Aircraft can fire all of their machine-guns or one other weapon. Each Infantry Teams can fire one of their weapons.

Flying Helicopters can only be shot at by:
- Anti-aircraft weapons (Dedicated AA, Guided AA, or weapons whoses name includes 'AA MG'),
- Anti-helicopter weapons,
- Guided weapons, or
- other Infantry Teams that are not using Heavy Weapons.

Landed Aircraft can be shot at by any weapon.

SHOOTING AT AIRCRAFT IN ENEMY TURN

You can either shoot at Aircraft in your own Shooting Step, or in the *enemy* Shooting Step immediately before the Aircraft shoots.

However, Guided weapons (other than Guided AA weapons) can only shoot at Aircraft in their own turn.

A weapon that shoots at Aircraft in the enemy Shooting Step cannot:
- Shoot at another Aircraft in this Shooting Step.
- Shoot in Defensive Fire in the Assault Step.
- Shoot in their own Shooting Step next turn.

In addition, the Team may not Assault in their Assault Step next turn and cannot be Gone to Ground until the end of the enemy's next turn.

You may find it useful to mark a Team that Shoots at aircraft in your opponent's turn.

Anti-aircraft token

SHOOTING AT FLYING AIRCRAFT

Anti-aircraft weapons like the ZSU-23-4 Shilka can shoot at any type of Aircraft in their own turn, or in the enemy turn immediately before the Aircraft shoot.

Tanks cannot normally shoot at flying Aircraft, except with their AA MG. However, the 30mm 2A42 gun on the BMP-2 is an Anti-helicopter weapon, so can shoot at Helicopters. Guided missiles like the AT-5 Sprandrel can also shoot at Helicopters in their own turn.

Infantry teams (aside from Heavy Weapons) can shoot at Helicopters, but not Strike Aircraft.

LINE OF SIGHT AND RANGE

A team must be in Range of, and be able to draw a Line of Sight to the target to shoot.

Missiles have a Minimum Range. Targets within this range cannot be shot at.

Tanks measure Range from any part of the Hull, but trace Line of Sight from the weapon mount.

1) CHECK RANGE

A weapon can only Shoot at a target within its Range. Measurements to and from an Infantry Team are made from the nearest edge of its base. Measurements to and from a Tank Team are made from the nearest part of its hull (ignoring weapons). Measurements to and from an Aircraft are made from the nearest part of its fuselage (ignoring wings, tails, helicopter rotors, and any weapons).

Weapons with a Minimum Range cannot hit a target where any part of it is within that distance.

2) CHECK LINE OF SIGHT

A Team can only shoot at a target within its Line of Sight. To establish Line of Sight, a player must trace an imaginary line from the shooting Team to any point on the target Team. The best way to do this is to get down to the level of the miniature and see what it could see.

Line of Sight is measured from:
- the weapon mounting of a Tank Team,
- any part of the base of an Infantry Team, or
- any point on the flight stand of an Aircraft.

Line of Sight is measured to:
- any point on a Tank Team (excluding weapons),
- anywhere on the base of an Infantry Team, or
- any point on the flight stand of an Aircraft.

Treat all the space that would be occupied by a standing figure anywhere on the base (as if the figures on the base stood up and moved around) as part of an Infantry Team. In essence, it is a block as tall as a standing miniature.

NO LINE OF SIGHT

Line of Sight is blocked by Tall Terrain (including Buildings and Hills) and friendly Teams (other than stationary Infantry Teams). A Team cannot shoot at a target if all (or practically all) of the Lines of Sight are blocked.

LINE OF SIGHT THROUGH GAPS

Gaps of less than ¾"/20mm between two terrain pieces or friendly Teams (other than stationary Infantry Teams) give Concealment and block Line of Sight in the same way that the terrain or Teams do.

Use a tape measure as a guide as to whether a gap is wide enough to see through.

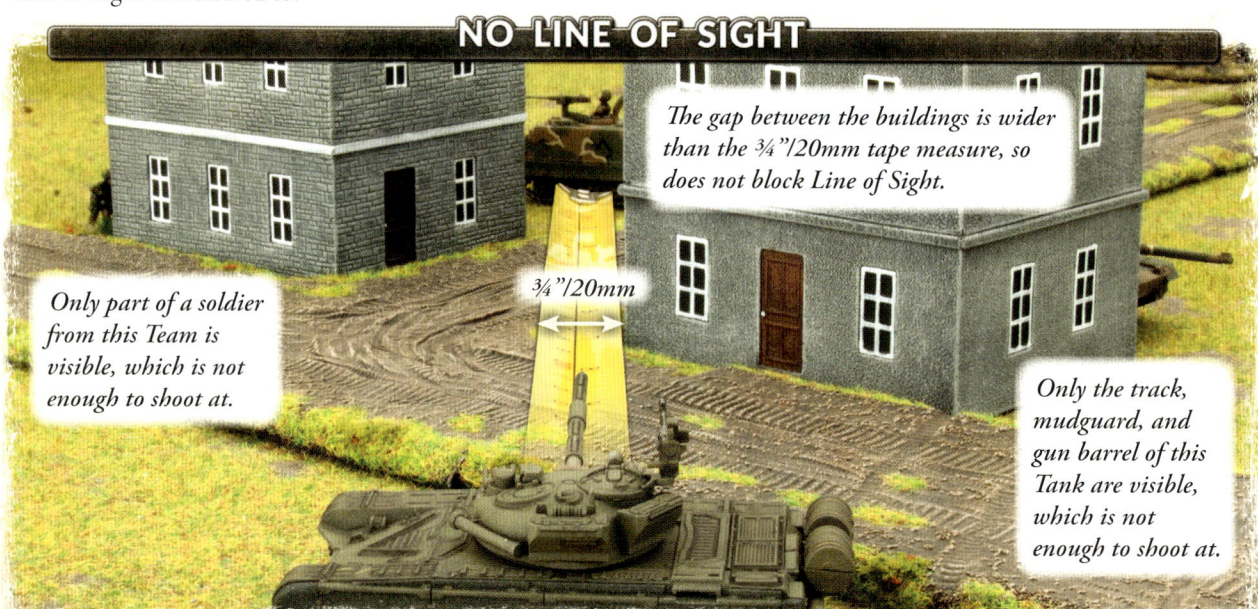

NO LINE OF SIGHT

The gap between the buildings is wider than the ¾"/20mm tape measure, so does not block Line of Sight.

Only part of a soldier from this Team is visible, which is not enough to shoot at.

Only the track, mudguard, and gun barrel of this Tank are visible, which is not enough to shoot at.

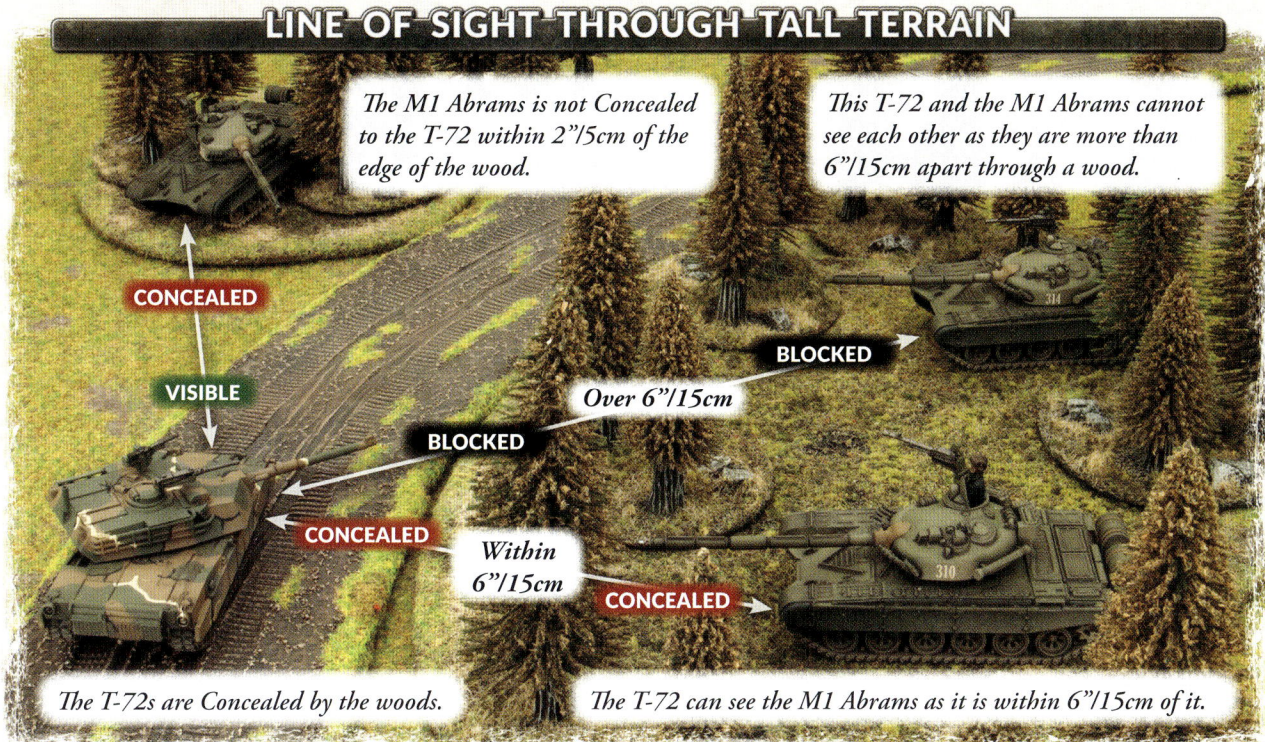

LINE OF SIGHT THROUGH TALL TERRAIN

Line of Sight to a target Team is Blocked if it is more than 2"/5cm through Tall Terrain, unless the Range is 6"/15cm or less.

LINE OF SIGHT THROUGH HILLS & BUILDINGS

Buildings and Hills block Line of Sight, so Teams completely behind them cannot be seen.

LINE OF SIGHT TO AND FROM AIRCRAFT

Terrain never blocks Line of Sight to or from Aircraft.

3) CHECK FOR CONCEALMENT

Teams that are concealed by terrain are harder to hit.

CONCEALED BY TALL OR SHORT TERRAIN

Short and Tall Terrain, other than Hills or Buildings, provides Concealment for Teams seen through it with the following exceptions:

- If the Shooting Team is within 2"/5cm of the edge of the Terrain, target Teams outside the terrain seen through that edge are not Concealed.
- If the Shooting Team is on higher ground, such as on a Hill or in the upper floor of a Building, or is an Aircraft, target Teams within or through Short Terrain are not Concealed.

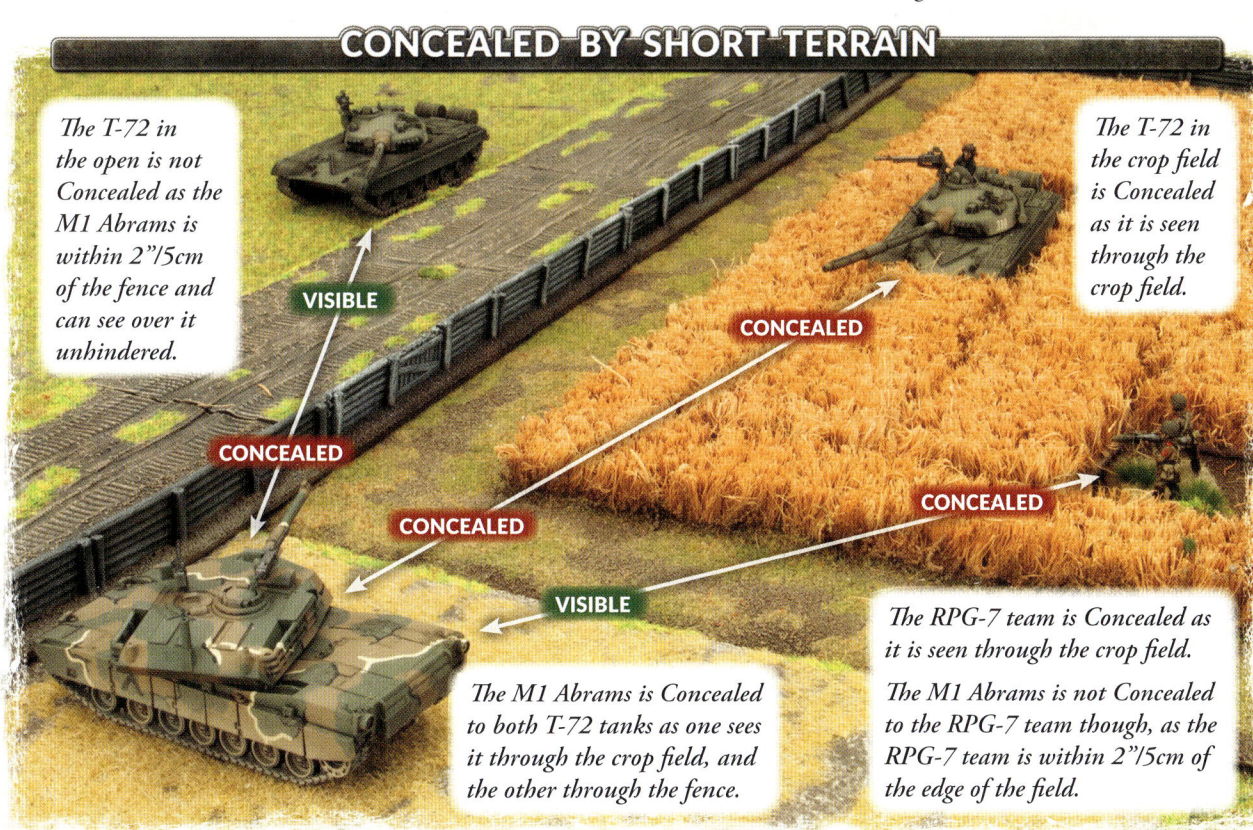

CONCEALED IN FLAT TERRAIN

Flat Terrain does not provide Concealment, except for Infantry Teams that did not move (even if they Dug In). These Teams are Concealed from all enemy Teams except Aircraft.

CONCEALED BY BUILDINGS

Buildings provide Concealment for Teams within them and for Teams at least half behind them.

CONCEALED BY HILLS

A Team half hidden by a Hill is Concealed to Teams on the other side, for example a tank with its hull hidden by the hill and its turret poking over ('hull down' as the military calls it). If it is high enough up the Hill, it will be able to see Teams on the other side clearly. The easiest way to determine Line of Sight and Concealment to and from a Hill is to physically get down to the level of the miniature and take a look at what the miniature could see from its current position.

CONCEALMENT AND AIRCRAFT

Only target Teams seen through Tall terrain (including Buildings, Hills, and Smoke) within 4"/10cm of the target Team are Concealed from Shooting Aircraft.

Aircraft are only Concealed if seen through Tall terrain (including Buildings, Hills, and Smoke) within 4"/10cm of the Shooting Team.

The exception is that Hunter-killer Helicopters gain Concealment from Tall terrain (including Buildings and Hills) within 4"/10cm of itself.

Line of Sight and Concealment for Landed Aircraft are treated the same way as any other Team on the ground.

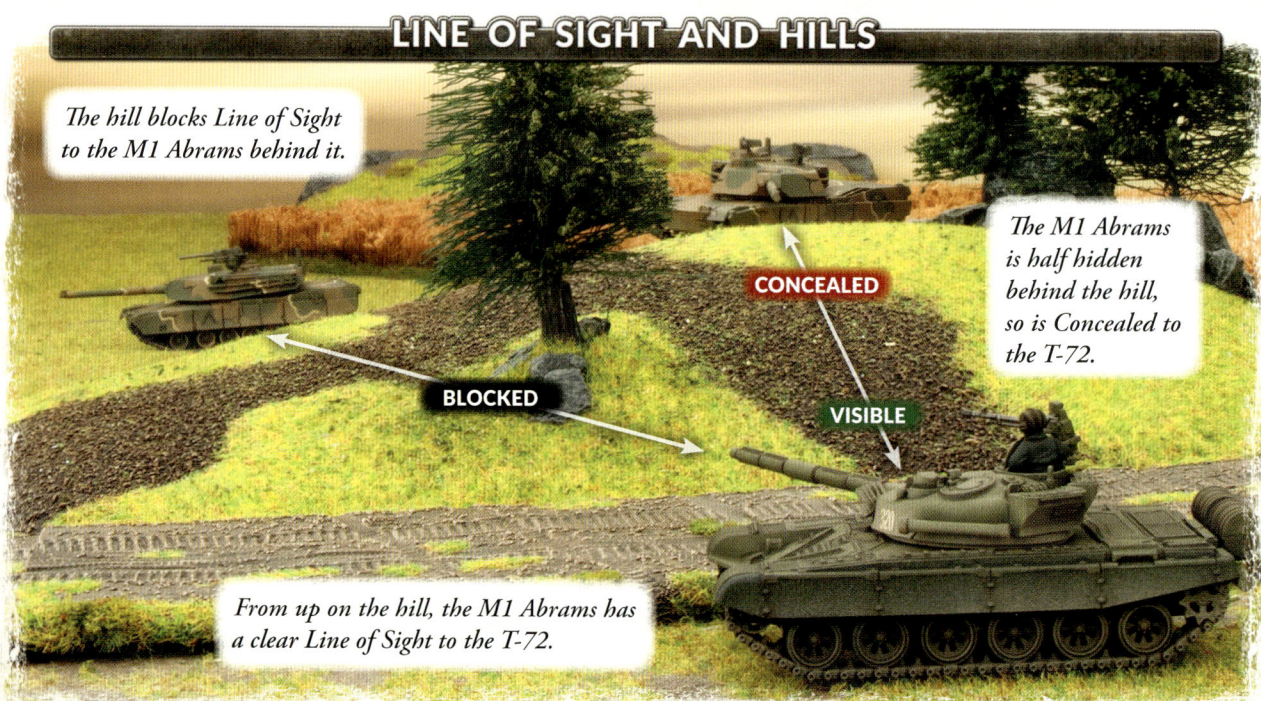

CONCEALMENT AND AIRCRAFT

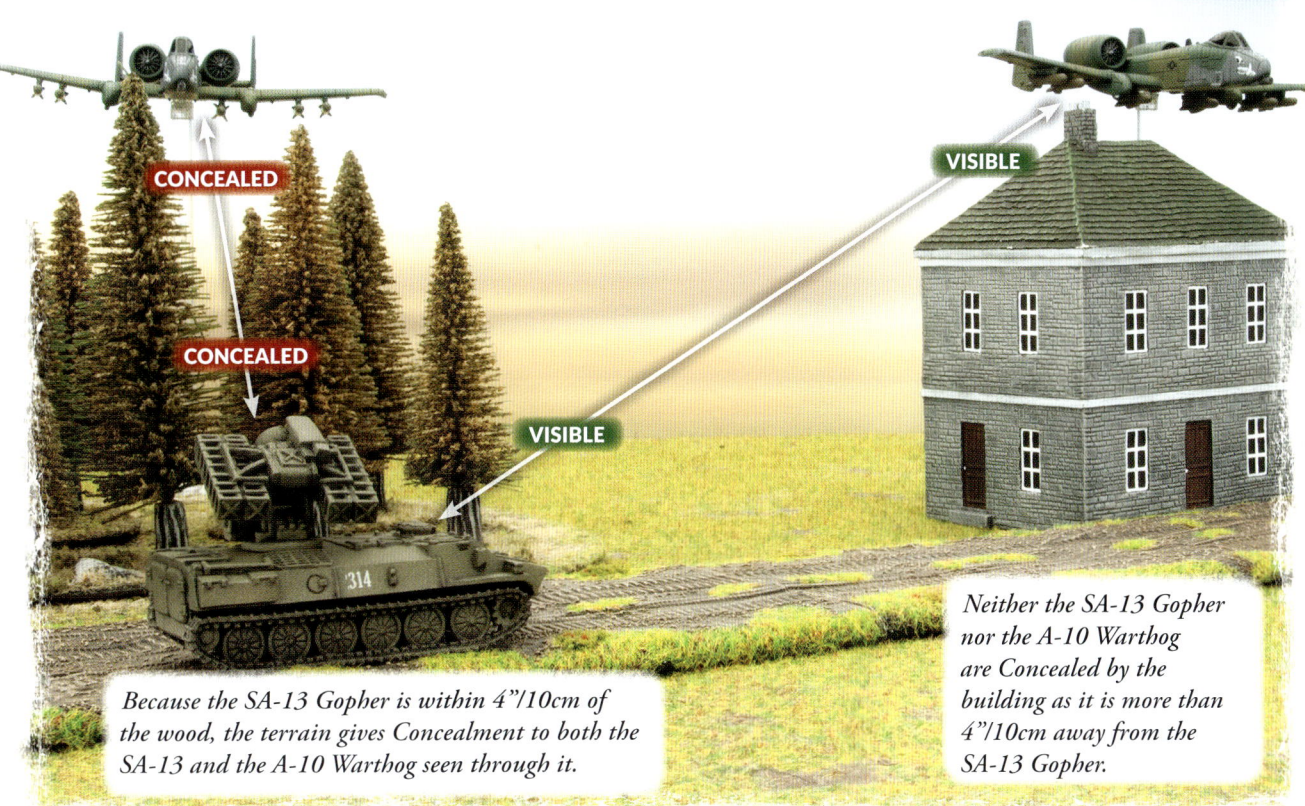

Because the SA-13 Gopher is within 4"/10cm of the wood, the terrain gives Concealment to both the SA-13 and the A-10 Warthog seen through it.

Neither the SA-13 Gopher nor the A-10 Warthog are Concealed by the building as it is more than 4"/10cm away from the SA-13 Gopher.

HUNTER-KILLER AIRCRAFT

As a Hunter-killer Helicopter, the Cobra is Concealed because it is within 4"/10cm of the building.
The ZSU-23-4 Shilka anti-aircraft tank is more than 4"/10cm away from the building, so is not concealed.

4) DECLARE TARGETS

After checking the Range and Line of Sight to potential targets, a player must declare an enemy Team as the target for each Team in the Unit. Multiple Teams can target a single enemy or you can spread your fire out as you wish.

A Team may only declare a single target Team, and all of its weapons will engage this target (although if it scores more than one hit, the additional hits may be placed on nearby Teams instead).

LIMITED FIELDS OF FIRE

Some weapons have a limited Field of Fire (see Forward Firing on page 66 as an example). They may only target or allocate hits to a Team within their Field of Fire.

Units can end their movement facing any direction, so when you move Units that have a limited Field of Fire, point them at their intended target.

AIRCRAFT SAFETY DISTANCE

Aircraft cannot target or allocate hits to a Tank or Infantry Team within 8"/20cm of a friendly Team.

5) ROTATE TO FACE

Rotate the Team to point its main weapon or weapons at the declared target Team. If the main weapon is mounted in a turret, you may rotate the whole model up to a quarter turn (90 degrees) to point at the target Team, rotating the turret, the rest of the way. Otherwise rotate the whole Team to point at the target Team. This is a free rotation as part of Shooting, and is not Movement.

6) ROLL TO HIT

Once you have declared targets for the Teams in a Unit, roll to hit the targets.

HOW MANY DICE?

Roll one die for each point of ROF. As shown on the Unit card, the ROF of a weapon changes depending on whether the Team is halted or Moved in the Movement Step.

If a Team is Pinned Down (page 50) or wishes to Assault later in the turn (page 57), it must Shoot with its Moving ROF.

A Team cannot Shoot if it moved at Dash speed, or used a Follow Me or Cross Here order (pages 36 to 37).

ANTI-AIRCRAFT FIRE

Dedicated AA, Guided AA, and Aircraft weapons use their full ROF when shooting at Aircraft. Other weapons shooting at flying Aircraft have ROF 1, and if they would normally have ROF 1, they suffer an additional +1 on their score to hit.

GONE TO GROUND

Teams that did not Move, Shoot, or Assault in their own turn and have not shot in this turn are Gone to Ground. Scouts can Move and still be Gone to Ground, but are not Gone to Ground if they Shoot or Assault (page 69). In addition, all Teams are Gone to Ground at the start of the game unless otherwise specified.

If a Team is Gone to Ground and is also Concealed from a Team Shooting at it, the Team is harder to hit.

SCORE TO HIT

The score To Hit is shown as the Is Hit On number on the **target Team's** Unit Card, modified as follows:

Add +1 to the score to hit for each of the following:
- The range to the targeted Team is over 16"/40cm.
- Target Team is Concealed (but not Gone to Ground).
- Shooting Team moved Out of Command.
- Shooting through Smoke.
- Shooting at Night.

Add +2 to the score to hit if:
- Target Team is Concealed and Gone to Ground.

TARGETS REQUIRING 7 OR MORE TO HIT

If the score needed to hit is 7 and the die roll is 6, then the shot scores a hit on a further roll of 5+.

If the score needed to hit is 8 and the die roll is 6, then the shot scores a hit on a further roll of 6.

If the score needed to hit is 9 or more, then the shot cannot hit.

SPEEDING THINGS UP

Shooting can involve lots of die rolls. Don't panic though—you don't always have to roll each die separately.

Because most Units have the same weapons in each Team and often all need the same score to hit, you can often (with your opponent's agreement) roll all the dice for a Unit's shooting at the same time, and assign the hits as normal.

In some cases however, taking it slowly and resolving the shooting one Team at a time makes complicated situations much simpler than they appear at first glance.

SCORE TO HIT

A BMP-1 platoon has moved into range of an M163 VADS, which opens up with its Vulcan Gatling gun's Halted ROF.

The M163 VADS needs to equal or exceed the targeted BMP-1's modified Is Hit On number in order to hit it. With four teams to choose from, it targets the closest one as the easiest to hit.

ASSIGN HITS

The M163 VADS scores four hits on the BMP-1 Platoon. All of them targeted at the closest tank.

1 The US player must assign the first hit against the targeted tank.

2 The US player must assign the remaining hits evenly to tanks from the platoon within 6"/15cm of the target.

3 The fourth tank is too far away, so they assign an additional hit to the second tank.

7) ASSIGN HITS

Once all of the Unit's Teams have rolled to hit, the shooting player assigns the hits from the shooting Unit. The hits must be assigned to Teams that are:

- a valid target for the Team that scored the hit,
- part of the same Unit as the target Team,
- of the same type (Tank, Infantry, or Aircraft) as the target Team, and
- within 6"/15cm of the target Team.

A target Team must be assigned at least one hit from the Team or Teams that targeted it. Hits from a weapon must be assigned evenly so that each Team has (as close as possible) the same number of hits from that type of weapon. The combined Hits from a Unit must also be assigned evenly.

HQ UNITS AND INDEPENDENT TEAMS

When an HQ Unit or Independent Team (such as an Observer) has been targeted, the Shooting player may select another Unit and assign hits between them as if they were the same Unit. Hits must still be assigned using the normal rules, and Teams from the other Unit must be of the same Type (Tank, Infantry, or Aircraft) as the target Team in order to be assigned a hit.

> ### DOING IT THE EASY WAY
> In most cases (especially if you targeted the Team in the middle of the enemy Unit), hit allocation comes down to placing one hit on the target Team, giving each of the Unit's Teams a hit until you run out of hits.

MISTAKEN TARGET

The targeted player may attempt to protect valuable Teams like heavy weapons by reassigning hits to other Teams representing misidentification of their target by the Shooting Team.

The player selects a Team that was hit and another Team of the same Type (Tank, Infantry, or Aircraft) that could have been assigned hits (whether it was or not) and rolls a die.

- On a roll of 3+, the player swaps all of the hits on each Team to the other Team. The hits must still be allocated according to the Assign Hits rule (page 45) after the swap. Once a hit has been swapped it cannot be swapped again. Any hits that cannot be legally swapped remain on the original Team.

If the player succeeds, they can then attempt to swap hits between a different pair of Teams, and continue to do so as long as they make the 3+ roll required. If they fail in any attempt to swap, all remaining hits stay where they were allocated.

TOO CLOSE FOR ERROR

The target player cannot use the Mistaken Target rule if the Shooting Team is:

- within 4"/10cm of either of the selected Teams, or
- within 8"/20cm if the selected Teams are Tank Teams.

HQ UNITS AND INDEPENDENT TEAMS

When an HQ Unit or Independent Team (such as an Observer) is hit, the owning player may select another Unit and use the Mistaken Target rule to swap hits between them as if they were the same Unit.

MISTAKEN TARGET

As the third tank is at long range, so less vulnerable to penetration (see Roll Saves on page 46), the Soviet player attempts to swap its hits with those on the second tank, needing to score 3+ to do so.

With a roll of 5, the Soviet player can swap all of the hits on the second tank for all of the hits on the third tank.

FRONT OR SIDE ARMOUR – TURRETLESS VEHICLES

This BMP-2 is entirely in front of a line drawn across the front of the Jaguar, which will use its Front armour rating for its Armour Save against its shooting.

This BMP-2 is at least partly behind the front of the Jaguar, which will use its Side armour rating for its Armour Saves.

8) ROLL SAVES

The targeted player rolls a save for each hit.

ARMOURED TANK TEAM SAVES

When the shooting player hits a turreted Tank Team, they first roll a die to determine whether the shot hits the hull or the turret.

- On a score of 4+, the shot hits the turret, if it has one.
- Otherwise, it hits the hull.

If the firing Team is entirely in front of a line drawn across the front of the hull or turret (whichever was hit), the opponent uses their Team's Front armour rating when rolling their Armour Save. Otherwise they use the Side armour rating.

If the firing Team is in the front or side of both the hull and turret, there is no need to roll to see which was hit.

NO NEED TO ROLL

If the Shooting Team is to the front or side of both the hull and turret (or you are shooting at a turretless tank), you do not need to roll to see which was hit as the Armour rating of both are the same.

ROLL SAVE

When an Armoured Tank Team is assigned a hit, the owning player takes an Armour Save. They roll a die and add:

- The Team's Armour rating.
- An additional +1 if the range between the Team that scored the hit and the Team making the save is over 16"/40cm.

EXCEEDS ANTI-TANK RATING

If your opponent's Armour Save roll is greater than your weapon's Anti-tank rating, their Armour Save is successful. The shot has no effect, having bounced harmlessly off the tank's armour.

FRONT OR SIDE ARMOUR – TURRETED VEHICLES

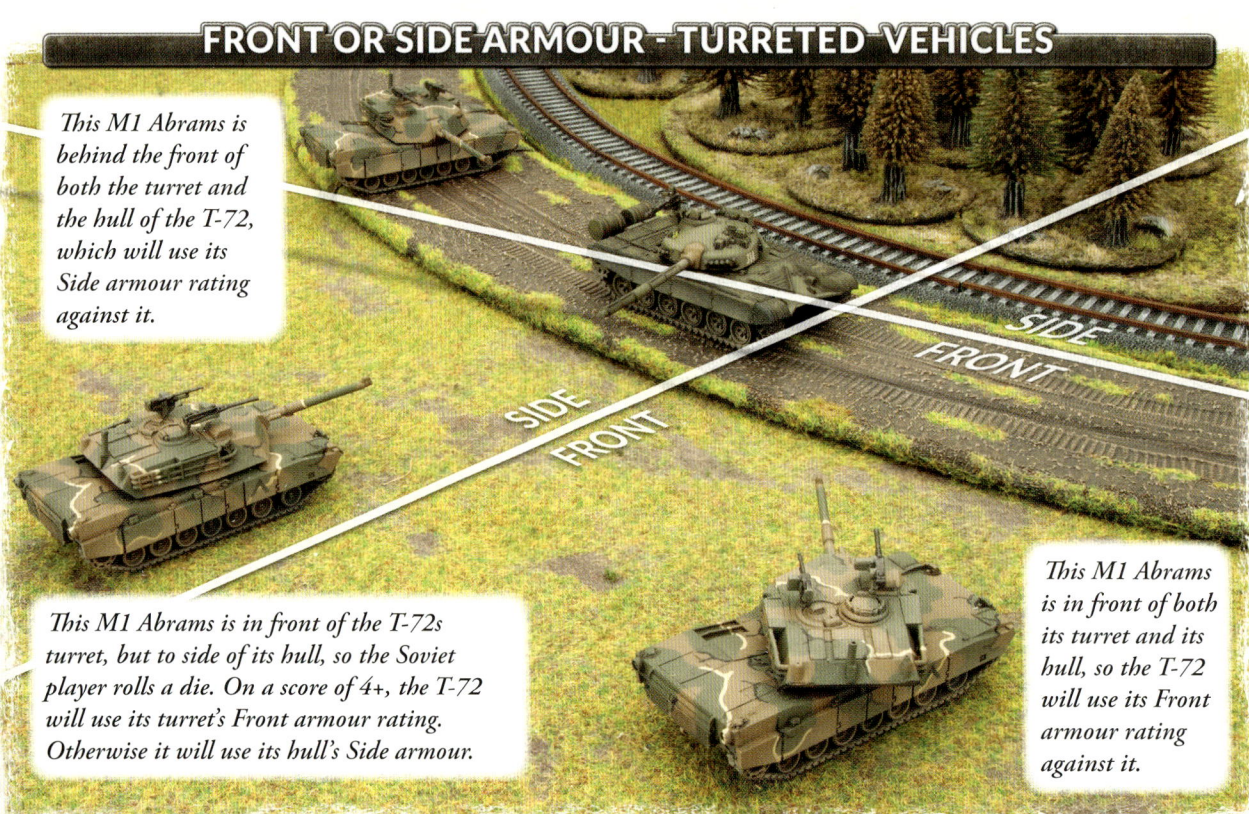

This M1 Abrams is behind the front of both the turret and the hull of the T-72, which will use its Side armour rating against it.

This M1 Abrams is in front of the T-72s turret, but to side of its hull, so the Soviet player rolls a die. On a score of 4+, the T-72 will use its turret's Front armour rating. Otherwise it will use its hull's Side armour.

This M1 Abrams is in front of both its turret and its hull, so the T-72 will use its Front armour rating against it.

EQUALS ANTI-TANK RATING

If your opponent's Armour Save roll exactly equals your weapon's Anti-tank rating, they failed their Armour Save. Although your shot didn't penetrate the tank's armour, it might still do some damage.

To determine the effect of the hit you must take a Firepower Test. Roll another die.

- If the roll equals or exceeds your weapon's Firepower rating, the crew panic and Bail Out.
- If the roll is lower than your weapon's Firepower rating the shot has no effect and the tank continues in action unharmed.

LESS THAN ANTI-TANK RATING

If your opponent's Armour Save roll is less than your weapon's Anti-tank rating they failed their Armour Save.

To determine the effect of the hit you must take a Firepower test. Roll another die.

- If the roll equals or exceeds your weapon's Firepower rating, the tank is Destroyed.
- If the roll is lower than your weapon's Firepower rating the shot failed to do significant damage to the tank but the crew still Bails Out of the tank fearing that the next shot might do worse.

ARMOURED VEHICLE SAVES

The M163 VADS Vulcan Gatling gun has an Anti-tank rating of 6 and a Firepower rating of 5+. The Soviet player rolls a Armour Save for each hit.

The first BMP-1 rolls a 5 and adds its armour rating of 2 for a total of 7. This is more than the M163 VADS' Anti-tank rating of 6, so the shot bounces off.

The second BMP-1 rolls a 1 and adds 2, giving a total of 3. This is less than the M163 VADS' Anti-tank rating, so the shot penetrates. If the M163 VADS scores its Firepower of 5+, the tank is Destroyed, otherwise it is Bailed Out.

The third BMP-1 rolls two 3's. Adding the armour rating of 2 and an additional +1 for range over 16"/40cm, this gives both dice a total of 6. This is equal to the M163's Anti-tank rating, so the shot may be effective. If the M163 scores its Firepower of 5+, the tank is Bailed Out. Otherwise it is unharmed.

If the M163 managed to Bail Out the tank twice, it must immediately roll its Remount number or be Destroyed.

BAILED OUT TANK TEAMS

Bailed Out Tank Teams may not move (including issuing Blitz Move, Shoot and Scoot, or Follow Me orders) or fight (including Shooting, firing Artillery Bombardments, and fighting in Assaults) until the crew Remount the tank.

BAILED OUT LEADERS AND COMMANDERS

If a Unit Leader or Formation Commander is Bailed Out they may, at the start of any Step, swap to another Tank Team within 6"/15cm that is under their command. Their Bailed Out Tank then replaces their new one in its original Unit.

BAILED OUT AGAIN

Each time a Tank Team that is already Bailed Out would be forced to Bail Out again (whether from Shooting or from Assault or any other reason), roll a die instead of placing another marker.

- If the score is greater than or equal to the Team's Remount, the shot has no additional effect on the tank.
- Otherwise, the crew decides that it's too dangerous to hang around, and the Team is Destroyed.

REMOUNTING BAILED OUT TANK TEAMS

During the Starting Step (page 29) at the start of your turn, roll a die for each Bailed Out Tank Team.

- If the score equals or exceeds the Tank Team's Remount rating, the crew Remounts their tank. The Team can now act as normal this turn.
- Otherwise, the Team remains Bailed Out.

COMMANDER'S LEADERSHIP

Re-roll all failed attempts to Remount for Tanks (including the Commander's own Tank) whose Commander is within 6"/15cm and in Line of Sight (ignoring friendly Teams).

INFANTRY SAVES

INFANTRY SAVE 3+

The M113 Mech Platoon took three hits. The Infantry teams roll an Infantry Save of 3+ for each hit.

The M249 SAW team fails its save and is Destroyed.

One of the M47 Dragon teams fails its save. As it is in Bulletproof Cover, the Soviet player needs to roll the shooting weapon's Firepower number or higher to Destroy it.

INFANTRY SAVES

For each hit on an enemy Infantry Team, the owning player rolls a die.
- If the result is at least the Team's Infantry Save, the Team survives largely unharmed.
- Otherwise, unless the Team is in Bulletproof Cover, it is Destroyed.

BULLETPROOF COVER

An Infantry Team that is in Foxholes or Concealed by a Building, Crater, Trench Line, Stone Wall, Bocage Hedgerow, Hill, or similar bulletproof terrain is in Bulletproof Cover.

The shooting player must roll a die for each unsaved hit on an Infantry Team in Bulletproof Cover.
- If the roll equals or exceeds the weapon's Firepower rating, the target Team is Destroyed.
- If the roll is lower than the weapon's Firepower rating, the cover protects the Team from harm.

UNARMOURED TANK SAVES

When an Unarmoured Tank Team (one with a Tank Save value instead of an Armour value) is assigned a hit, the owning player rolls a die.
- If the result is at least the Team's Unarmoured Tank Save, the tank survives unharmed apart from some holes in the bodywork.
- Otherwise, it is Destroyed.

AIRCRAFT SAVES

When an Aircraft is assigned a hit, the owning player rolls a die.
- If the result is at least the Team's Aircraft Save, the aircraft survives unharmed apart from some holes in the wings.
- Otherwise, the shooting player must roll a die for each unsaved hit.
  - If the roll equals or exceeds the weapon's Firepower rating, the target Aircraft is Destroyed.
  - Otherwise, the Aircraft survives unharmed and continues its attack.

AIRCRAFT SAVES

AIRCRAFT SAVE 4+

The Mi-24 Hind takes a hit from the M113s .50 cal AA MG, so the Soviet player rolls an Aircraft save.

On a roll of 4+, the Mi-24 Hind would be unharmed. Otherwise, the US player must roll against the .50 cal's Firepower of 5+ to Destroy it, rerolling a successful attempt.

The Mi-24 Hind then takes a hit from the M249 SAW team. With a score of 2, the Soviet player fails their Aircraft Save. The US player rolls a 6 for their Firepower, but since the M249 SAW team is an Infantry team, they must re-roll their success. Their second roll is a 1, so the Mi-24 Hind survives.

DESTROYED ARMOURED VEHICLES

Mark Destroyed Tanks and Landed Aircraft as Wrecks.

Wrecks are Terrain, so slow movement and provide Concealment. Wrecks of Armoured Tanks are also Bulletproof Cover.

DESTROYED TEAMS

Leave Destroyed Tank and Landed Aircraft Teams on the table as Wrecks. Remove all Destroyed Infantry and flying Aircraft Teams from the table.

Mark a wreck by placing a plume of smoke on the model representing smoke and flame from internal fires. Wrecks are Terrain, slowing down tanks dashing across them, but are not Difficult Terrain. Wrecks (ignoring the smoke plume) provide Concealment as Short Terrain. Armoured Tank team Wrecks are Bulletproof Cover.

PASSENGERS IN DESTROYED TRANSPORTS

When a Team carrying Passengers is Destroyed, consult the rules on page 35 to find the effect on the Passengers.

REPLACE DESTROYED UNIT LEADERS

When a Unit Leader is Destroyed, the next in line for command takes over.

If a Unit Leader is Destroyed, nominate another Team of the same Type from the Unit within 6"/15cm as the new Unit Leader Team.

If there are no suitable Teams close enough, the Unit remains leaderless until the Leader is replaced. A Formation Commander may appoint another Team from the Unit within 6"/15cm and in Line of Sight as the new Unit Leader at the start of any of their turns.

KILLING COMMANDERS

When a Formation Commander is Destroyed the owning player can nominate another Team of the same type from the HQ Unit within 6"/15cm as the new Formation Commander.

If they cannot do this, the owning player rolls a die.

- On a roll of 3+, the Commander survives and switches to another Team if there is one available. If there are no Teams of the appropriate Type within 6"/15cm, the Commander is killed.
- Otherwise, the Commander is killed.

SWITCHING TO ANOTHER TEAM

If your Infantry Commander survives, remove another friendly Infantry Team from their Formation within 6"/15cm and replace it with the Commander's Team.

If your Tank Commander survives, nominate another friendly Tank Team from their Formation within 6"/15cm as the new Commander. The Commander now uses the characteristics from the new Tank Team's card.

ONLY ROLL ONCE

If a Commander is Destroyed multiple times by a Unit's Shooting, the Commander still only needs to roll once to see if they survive.

KEEPING TRACK OF LEADERS

It is a good idea to make your leaders easy to identify with different markings or a commander model for tanks. For infantry your Unit Leader will have a officer and a radio operator.

If your leader is Destroyed, it is usually a good idea to pick a team with the same characteristics to be the new leader and then just swap the old leader for it. That way they are still easy to identify.

If your new leader is in a different type of tank or is armed with a different weapon, you can use a Leader token to keep track of them instead if you want.

Leader token

PINNED DOWN PLATOONS

The M113 Mech Platoon took seven hits. As an Infantry Unit, it is Pinned Down because it took at least five hits.

Until the company Rallies, its teams cannot move toward visible enemy teams.

Teams that shoot while Pinned Down, must do so using their Moving ROF, whether they move or not.

PINNED DOWN

Even if you don't manage to kill the enemy with your Shooting, the weight of fire may pin them down. For soldiers under such intense fire, forward progress is impossible, and even shooting is difficult.

- A Unit becomes Pinned Down if it takes at least five hits in a single Shooting Step. These hits can be from any source or combination of sources, as long as all of the hits were inflicted in the same Shooting Step.
- A larger Unit that started the Shooting Step with at least twelve Teams needs to take at least eight hits in the Shooting Step to become Pinned Down.

INFANTRY AND UNARMOURED TEAMS

Infantry and Unarmoured Tank Teams in a Pinned Down Unit may not Move closer to any enemy Team in Line of Sight, nor Move into Line of Sight of any other enemy Team. However, they may Dig In or retire away from visible enemy Teams.

A Pinned Down Infantry or Unarmoured Tank Team Shoots using its Moving ROF, whether it Moved or not.

ARMOURED TANK TEAMS AND AIRCRAFT

Armoured Tank Teams, Passenger Teams mounted in an Armoured Transport, and Aircraft cannot be Pinned Down.

RALLYING FROM PINNED DOWN

If your Unit is Pinned Down, you may attempt to Rally it in the Starting Step at the start of your turn. Roll a die to do so:

- If the score is greater than or equal to the Rally rating, the Unit recovers fully and is immediately ready to continue the battle.
- Otherwise, the Unit remains Pinned Down.

COMMANDER'S LEADERSHIP

Re-roll all failed attempts to Rally from Pinned Down for Units (including the Commander's own HQ Unit) whose Commander is within 6"/15cm and in Line of Sight (ignoring intervening friendly troops) of the Unit Leader.

FIRING SMOKE

Before Shooting normally, a Unit may elect to fire Smoke, rather than armour-piercing or explosive ammunition, with any or all of its weapons that have this capability. These Teams cannot Shoot after doing this.

When a Team fires Smoke, each hit places a 2"/5cm Smoke marker (or ball of cotton wool) on the Team rather than causing any direct damage. Hits by Smoke cannot be reallocated with the Mistaken Target rule.

All Smoke fired by a player is removed at the start of their next turn.

EFFECTS OF SMOKE

Teams Shooting into, through, or out of a Smoke ball always suffer an additional +1 penalty on the score needed to hit, both for Shooting and Bombardments, unless the shooting Team has Thermal Imaging.

If a Team that has been hit by Smoke moves, the Smoke remains in place, allowing the Team to Shoot as normal.

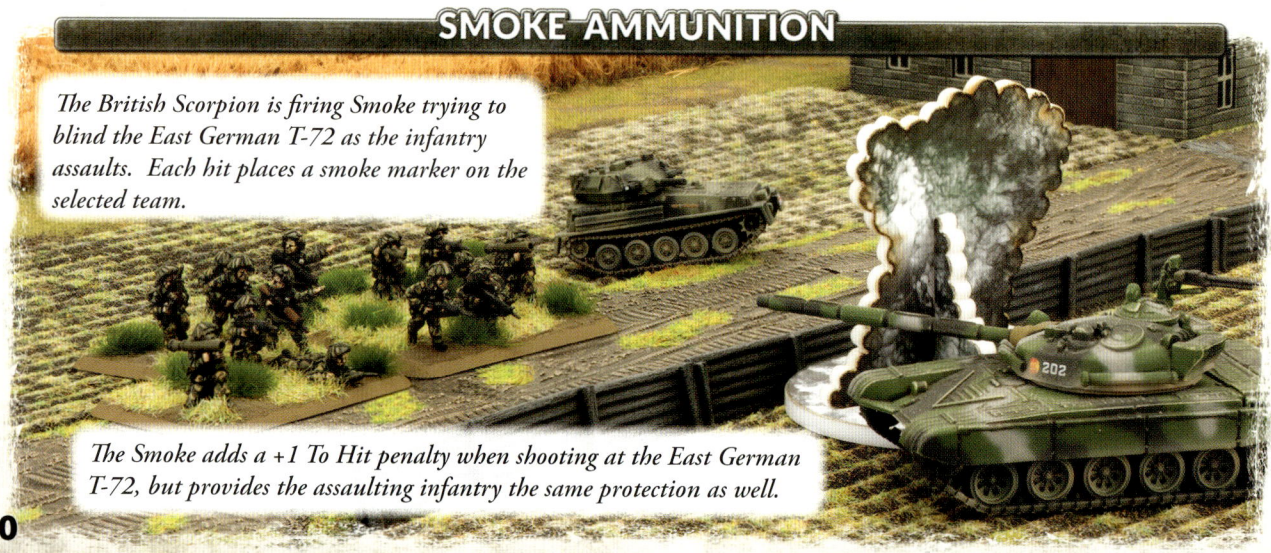

SMOKE AMMUNITION

The British Scorpion is firing Smoke trying to blind the East German T-72 as the infantry assaults. Each hit places a smoke marker on the selected team.

The Smoke adds a +1 To Hit penalty when shooting at the East German T-72, but provides the assaulting infantry the same protection as well.

ARTILLERY

He wanted the artillery to impact along the crest of the opposite hill at the same time the Team began to fire. First, DPICM, an artillery shell that scattered many small armor-defeating bomblets, would be fired in order to take out as many Soviet PCs and self-propelled guns as possible. Then the artillery would fire high explosives and smoke rounds, laying down a smoke screen to blind any Soviet anti-tank system or artillery observers that might take up position there to engage the Team. That would leave the Team free to slug it out with only a portion of their force isolated from the rest. The FSO assured Bannon the artillery could handle the mission. All he needed was the word.

ARTILLERY SEQUENCE

Artillery weapons are designed to bombard an area with a deluge of explosive shells rather than attempting to hit a particular target directly.

1. Pick Spotting Team *(see page 51)*
2. Check Range *(see page 51)*
3. Select Aiming Point *(see page 52)*
4. Rotate to Face *(see page 53)*
5. Roll to Range In *(see page 53)*
6. Roll to Hit *(see page 53)*
7. Roll Saves *(see page 54)*
8. Pin Down Target *(see page 54)*

WHO CAN BOMBARD

Any Team that has an Artillery weapon (indicated by a ROF of 'ARTILLERY' or 'SALVO') may fire a Bombardment instead of Shooting. A Unit with Artillery weapons is an Artillery Unit.

Most Artillery weapons have both a normal shooting line and an artillery line on their Unit Card. You must choose to use one or the other each turn. Some, like rocket launchers, can only fire bombardments and cannot shoot normally.

Teams cannot fire a Bombardment if they Moved (unless they are Aircraft), failed a Blitz Move order, attempted to Dig In, are in a Building, or are Pinned Down. Teams that fire a Bombardment cannot Assault this turn.

If a Unit fires a Bombardment, all of its Teams with Artillery weapons must either fire as part of the Bombardment, or not fire at all. Other Teams can still Shoot as normal.

1) PICK SPOTTING TEAM

An Artillery Bombardment needs a Team to Spot the fall of shot and correct the guns on to target. A Spotting Team can be one of the firing Teams, a Unit Leader, any Formation HQ Team, or a specialist Observer.

A Spotting team must not have Moved or attempted to Dig In, cannot Shoot or Assault, but can fire in the Bombardment it is Spotting for.

SPOTTING FOR AIRCRAFT

An Artillery Bombardment from an Aircraft Unit can only be Spotted for by one of the Aircraft in the Unit. Aircraft can spot for their own Bombardment while moving.

2) CHECK RANGE

Weapons can only fire a Bombardment at an Aiming Point within their Range and in their Field of Fire.

SPOTTING TEAM

Artillery units can select any point on the table that their Spotting Team can see as their Aiming Point.

SELECT TEMPLATE SIZE AND AIMING POINT

An M109 Field Artillery Battery is going to bombard the T-72 Tank Company using an Artillery Template.

If they fired Bomblet ammunition they would use the larger Salvo Template, would be less destructive.

The US player places the Aiming Point in the centre of the target to catch as many T-72 tanks as possible.

The sides of the Template point back to the bombarding unit.

3) SELECT AIMING POINT

Pick a point on the table within Line of Sight of the Spotting Team and place the firing Unit's Ranged In marker on it to mark it as the Aiming Point of the Bombardment.

Centre the Template over the Aiming Point with the sides pointing towards the Bombarding Unit.

TEMPLATE SIZE

The Artillery Template is 6"/15cm square, while the Salvo Template is 10"/25cm square.

DANGER CLOSE

The US player can't place the Template to hit the right-hand T-72 tank because that would bring the Template within 4"/10cm of their own infantry.

RANGING IN

The M109 Field Artillery Battery has a Skill number of 4+. It may make up to three attempts to Range In.

COURAGE 4+ — SKILL 4+
MORALE 4+ — ASSAULT 5+

The more attempts it takes to Range In, the less accurate its bombardment will be (see Roll To Hit on page 54).

First attempt — Second attempt — Third attempt

DANGER CLOSE

To reflect the danger of dropping shells too close to your own positions, you may not place an Artillery Template within 4"/10cm of friendly Teams, nor a Salvo Template within 6"/15cm of friendly Teams.

Aircraft may not place an Artillery or Salvo Template within 8"/20cm of friendly Teams, but do not restrict the placement of their own Template.

4) ROTATE TO FACE

The Artillery Teams Rotate to Face the Aiming Point. This is a free rotation as part of Shooting, and is not Movement.

If the Aiming Point is outside of the weapon's Field of Fire, it cannot fire as part of the Bombardment, but it still rotates to point at the Aiming Point.

5) ROLL TO RANGE IN

A Spotting Team can make up to three attempts to Range In the artillery on its Aiming Point. Roll a die for each attempt:

- If the score is greater than or equal to the Artillery Unit's Skill rating, it has successfully Ranged In.
- Otherwise, the ranging attempt missed, go on to the next attempt.

If the Spotting Team fails all three attempts to Range In, remove the Ranged In marker. The Artillery Unit that was attempting to Range In cannot Shoot, Assault, or fire an Artillery Bombardment this turn, and are not Gone to Ground.

Once a Spotting team has made their three attempts to Range In, they cannot make further Ranging In attempts this turn.

RANGING IN WITH A LESS-SKILLED TEAM

If the Spotting Team and the Artillery Unit have different Skill ratings (or Ranging ratings if they have them), use the worse rating to Range In.

RANGING IN WITH SPECIALIST OBSERVER

A specialist Observer Team reduces the score required to Range In by -1 (see page 69).

RANGING IN AN ADDITIONAL BATTERY

If the Spotting Team successfully Ranges In in less than three attempts, it may use its remaining attempts to Range In another Artillery Unit that it can Spot for on the same or a different Aiming Point. This Artillery Unit will suffer the normal penalty for Ranging In on the second or third attempt.

RANGING IN NEAR TERRAIN

Add +1 to the score required to Range In if the Aiming Point is placed so that the Template will cover any Short or Tall Terrain features or any part of a Smoke Screen.

RANGING IN AT NIGHT

A Spotting Team does not need to roll on the Night Visibility Table (page 84) when Spotting for a Bombardment at Night, but does add +1 to the score required to Range In. This is in addition to any penalty for Ranging In near Terrain.

6) ROLL TO HIT

Roll a die for each Tank or Infantry Team caught at least partly under the Template.

The score To Hit a Team under the Template is shown as the Is Hit On number on the target Team's Unit Card, modified as follows:

- Add +1 if Ranged In on the Second Attempt.
- Add +2 if Ranged In on the Third Attempt.

1 OR 2 WEAPONS FIRING

If the Artillery Unit only has one or two weapons firing, you must re-roll successful rolls To Hit.

5 OR MORE WEAPONS FIRING

If the Artillery Unit has five or more weapons firing, you must re-roll failed rolls To Hit.

ROLL TO HIT AND ROLL SAVES

The M109 Field Artillery Battery Ranges In on its third attempt.

The US player rolls one die for each T-72 tank under the Template.

The score to Hit is the T-72 tanks' Is Hit On number of 3+, with +2 penalty for taking two attempts to Range In, giving a score needed of 5+.

Since there are six guns firing, the US Player will re-roll any unsuccessful rolls To Hit.

The T-72 tanks use their Top armour for their Armour Saves against Artillery.

7) ROLL SAVES

Roll Saves for Teams that have been hit in the same way as for Shooting (pages 46 to 48), except that Armoured Tank Teams use their Top armour rating and do not have a bonus for ranges over 16"/40cm.

BULLETPROOF COVER AND BOMBARDMENTS

An Infantry Team that is in Foxholes or in a Building, Crater, or similar bulletproof terrain is in Bulletproof Cover. Teams behind Stone Walls, Bocage Hedgerows, and similar linear terrain are not in Bulletproof Cover from an Artillery Bombardment.

The shooting player must roll a die for each unsaved hit on an Infantry Team in Bulletproof Cover.
- If the roll equals or exceeds the weapon's Firepower rating, the target Team is Destroyed.
- If the roll is lower than the weapon's Firepower rating, the cover protects the Team from harm.

8) PIN DOWN TARGET

Infantry and Unarmoured Tank Units hit by an Artillery Bombardment are automatically Pinned Down (page 50).

REPEATING BOMBARDMENTS

An Artillery Unit may Repeat a Bombardment in a later turn using its current Aiming Point. Because the Artillery Unit is already Ranged In on that Aiming Point, it automatically Ranges In on its first attempt for the Repeated Bombardment, so will not suffer the penalty for Ranging In on the second or third attempt.

SPOTTING FOR A REPEAT BOMBARDMENT

The Repeated Bombardment still requires a Spotting Team, but it may be a different Team from the one that originally Ranged In on the Aiming Point and doesn't need to be able to see the Aiming Point.

If the Spotting Team cannot see the Aiming Point, all rolls To Hit will suffer a +1 penalty to the score required To Hit as if the Spotting Team had Ranged In on the second attempt.

RE-ROLL INFANTRY SAVES

Infantry Teams must re-roll successful Saves when hit by a Repeat Bombardment.

MOVING REMOVES RANGED IN MARKER

If an Artillery Unit moves (including when it uses a Blitz Move or Shoot and Scoot), it immediately removes its Ranged In marker from the table. Since Aircraft must move every turn, they will always remove their Ranged In marker between Bombardments.

PRE-PLANNED ARTILLERY TARGETS

An Artillery Unit that is not in Reserve may place its Ranged In marker anywhere on the table at the start of the game after Objectives and Minefields have been placed, but before Deployment. This Ranged In marker indicates the Artillery Unit's current Aiming Point at the start of the game.

If both sides have Artillery, the Defender places their Ranged In markers first.

Ranged In Marker

SPECIAL ARTILLERY AMMUNITION

Amidst the noise of the Soviet artillery fire that continued to pound Langen, the U.S. artillery-delivered mines arrived almost unnoticed. That is, until Soviet tanks began to run over them. As tanks began to hit the mines, shedding tracks severed by the detonation and stopping. Company and battalion commanders were confused. Buttoned up and with limited visibility, they at first thought they were under fire and took to searching for the telltale flashes of tank fire or the back blast of anti-tank missile launchers. All the while more tanks hit the mines, stopping them and causing other tanks to slow down or swerve left or right to avoid colliding with disabled tanks in front of them. Belatedly, it occurred to them they were in a minefield.

With the Soviets thrashing about in the open, Jordan directed the artillery to switch to firing dual-purpose improved conventional ammunition, or DPICM. Like the scatterable mine, the artillery projectiles were loaded with small submunitions. The submunitions in DPICM, however, were bomblets that exploded on contact and were designed to penetrate the thin armor covering the top of armored vehicles.

MINELETS

Minelet rounds such as FASCAM (Family of Scatterable Mines) are artillery shells filled with small mines. An artillery bombardment can create a minefield on the fly.

Once per game an Artillery Unit may fire Minelet ammunition rather than a normal Artillery Bombardment. If they do this, Range in the Artillery Bombardment as normal (see page 53). Once Ranged In, place one Minefield marker (see page 67) within 2"/5cm of the Aiming Point for every three weapons firing. The Artillery Bombardment has no other effect.

BOMBLETS

Bomblet rounds or DPICM (Dual-purpose Improved Conventional Munitions) are artillery shells packed with small explosive charges that they scatter over a wide area.

A Spotting Team can request a suitably-equipped Artillery Unit to fire Bomblets. When firing Bomblet ammunition, an artillery weapon has the following characteristics.

RANGE	ROF HALTED	ROF MOVING	ANTI-TANK	FIRE-POWER
NORMAL	SALVO	-	3	6

LASER-GUIDED PROJECTILES

Cannon-Launched Guided Projectiles like M712 Copperhead are artillery shells that can be guided on to the target by a laser-equipped observer.

Any Observer Team can request a suitably-equipped Artillery Unit to fire Laser-Guided Projectiles instead of firing an Artillery Bombardment.

The Artillery Unit must be capable of firing an Artillery Bombardment, but fires one Laser-Guided Projectile for each weapon firing instead, using the normal Shooting rules.

The key difference from normal shooting is that the Artillery Battery uses the Observer Team to determine its Line Of Sight, rather than its own position.

Weapons firing Laser-Guided Projectiles have the following characteristics.

RANGE	ROF HALTED	ROF MOVING	ANTI-TANK	FIRE-POWER	NOTES
16"/40CM—NORMAL	1	-	21	2+	Brutal, Guided, HEAT

GUIDED PROJECTILES

The M113 FIST requests Laser-Guided Projectiles instead of a bombardment.

The M109 howitzers can't see the target, but that doesn't matter as Line of Sight is taken from the M113 FIST.
The howitzers roll a die each to hit, using the normal shooting rules.

The projectiles will hit the tanks' Front armour since they are coming from the direction of the Artillery Battery.

SMOKE BOMBARDMENTS

To Bannon's surprise, another Soviet artillery unit began to lay down a massive smoke screen just in front of the Team's positions. They were going to attack soon. Bannon had expected the Soviets to wait until night to attack. But apparently they were being pushed by their commanders to break through and could not wait. Not that night would have made much of a difference. The gunners in the tank platoons and those manning the Dragons in the Mech Platoon were already switching to their thermal sights. The smoke screen the Soviet gunners were arduously building would offer the attacking force scant protection, if any.

SMOKE BOMBARDMENTS

Some Artillery Units can fire a Smoke Bombardment instead of a normal Artillery Bombardment. Each such Artillery Unit may do this once per game.

Smoke Bombardments must be fired at the beginning of the Shooting Step before all other fire.

Use the normal Artillery rules to Range In, except that there is no modifier for Ranging In near Terrain and no Danger Close restriction. If the Bombardment is successfully Ranged In, place a Smoke Screen on the Aiming Point. The Bombardment has no other effect. If the Unit fails to Range In, they may attempt to fire a Smoke Bombardment again later in the game.

All Smoke fired by a player is removed at the start of their next turn.

SMOKE SCREENS

When a Unit fires a Smoke Bombardment, place a line of 2"/5cm Smoke markers (or balls of cotton wool) that is 4"/10cm long for each weapon firing as a Smoke Screen. So two guns will produce a line 8"/20cm long, while four guns will produce a line 16"/40cm long. The line starts at the Aiming Point and may be placed on any angle. You may fire fewer weapons to produce a shorter screen if you wish.

EFFECTS OF SMOKE SCREENS

Lines of Sight into, through, or out of Smoke Screens are blocked unless the Range is 6"/15cm or less.

Teams shooting through or into a Smoke Screen always suffer an additional +1 penalty on the score needed To Hit for Shooting and on the score needed to Range In Bombardments, unless the shooting Team has Thermal Imaging.

SMOKE SCREENS

A 2S1 Carnation SP Howitzer Battery of three guns fires a Smoke Bombardment to screen the East German T-72 tanks from flanking fire by the German Leopard 1 tanks.

12"/30cm for three weapons

Because the Range is more than 6"/15cm, the German Leopard 1 will have to move if they want to shoot at the T-72 tanks.

The 2S1 Carnations successfully Range In, so the East German player places 12"/30cm (4"/10cm per gun) of smoke screen on

ASSAULTS

Two men stationed themselves on either side of the door. This time, the third man leaned over and threw a grenade into the opened door. As soon as the grenade went off, Polgar and the man across from him went charging into the house, guns leveled and blazing away. Polgar signaled for the third man to enter and cover him as he approached the stairs. He slowly began to climb the stairs, always peering up to see over onto the second floor. When he was halfway up the stairs, Polgar halted, took a grenade off of his web gear, pulled the pin, and threw it into the room at the head of the stairs. As soon as this grenade detonated, he charged to the top of the stairs, taking two steps at a time and firing as he went.

ASSAULT SEQUENCE

In the Assault Step, you assault with any or all of your Units one by one. When a Unit Assaults, its Teams move into contact, the enemy shoots defensive fire, then both sides take turns at fighting at close quarters with hand grenades and close-combat weapons.

Once you've finished assaulting with one of your Units, move on to the next, until all of the Units have made their assaults.

1. Charge into Contact *(see page 57)*
2. Opponent's Defensive Fire *(see page 59)*
3. Roll to Hit *(see page 60)*
4. Roll Saves *(see page 61)*
5. Check if the Assault is Over *(see page 61)*
6. Test to Counterattack *(see page 62)*
7. Counterattack or Break Off *(see pages 62 to 63)*

An Assault is the only time an Infantry Team can Move within 2"/5cm of the enemy, or that a Tank Team can Move within 2"/5cm of enemy Infantry Teams.

SHOOTING BEFORE ASSAULTING

A Team can shoot in the Shooting Step (but not fire an Artillery Bombardment) before Assaulting in the Assault Step. If it does so, it must use its Moving ROF (whether it moves or not), and must target a Team within 8"/20cm of the Team it will Charge into Contact with when it Assaults.

WHO CAN ASSAULT

In the Assault Step, an Armoured Tank Team or an Infantry Team can Assault if it is not:
- Pinned Down, or
- a Heavy Weapon,

and it did not:
- Move at Dash speed,
- Move more than 10"/25cm at Tactical speed,
- Use a Movement Order other than Follow Me,
- Shoot at its Halted ROF,
- Spot for or Fire an Artillery or Smoke Bombardment, or
- Shoot at Aircraft in the previous enemy turn,

and its Unit has not already Assaulted this turn.

LEADING FROM THE FRONT

A Formation Commander and their HQ Unit can combine with a Unit from their Formation to conduct a joint assault. To do this, the Formation Commander and the Unit Leader must be of the same Type (Tank or Infantry) and must start the Assault Step within 6"/15cm and in Line of Sight of each other. For the duration of the Assault Step, the combined Unit is treated as a single Unit having the worse of the two Units' Counterattack values.

1) CHARGE INTO CONTACT

An Assaulting Unit Moves any of its Tank or Infantry Teams up to 4"/10cm into Contact with an enemy Team by the shortest route. These Teams are now Assaulting Teams.

A Team is in Contact with an enemy Team if:
- its front edge is as close as it can get to the enemy Team, or
- it is an Infantry Team and its front edge is as close as it can get to another Infantry Team from its own Unit that is directly in Contact with an enemy Team.

Tank Teams cannot Assault other Tank Teams, so they cannot Charge into Contact with enemy Tank Teams. Heavy Weapons, Independent Teams, and Unarmoured Tank Teams cannot Charge into Contact at all.

Teams that can't Contact an enemy Team cannot Assault.

CHARGE INTO CONTACT

To launch an Assault, move your Teams in two steps.

Heavy Weapons cannot Charge into Contact.

First, move all Assaulting Teams that can directly contact enemy teams up to 4"/10cm into Contact, or as close as they can get.

An Assaulting Team must use its Moving ROF in the Shooting Step, and must Contact a team within 8"/20cm of the team it shot at. Teams that cannot make contact cannot charge and remain out of the assault.

Then, move any other Assaulting Infantry Teams that can Contact an Infantry Team in direct Contact up to 4"/10cm.

ASSAULTING THROUGH TERRAIN

If a Tank Team fails a roll to Cross terrain while moving into contact with the enemy, they halt their movement. If a Team was within 2"/5cm of an enemy Team when they failed the roll, move it back 2"/5cm from the enemy to indicate that it did not succeed in Charging into Contact.

Teams cannot Assault enemy troops that are in or across terrain that is Impassable to them.

If the Assaulting Team successfully Charged into Contact, but cannot be placed into Contact with an enemy Team because of a line of terrain, place it immediately across the terrain from the enemy and treat it as being in Contact.

ASSAULTING ACROSS OBSTACLES

The T-72 tanks launch an Assault against the US infantry across the hedge.

This T-72 failed its Cross Check, so stops 2"/5cm away from the obstacle.

This T-72 passed its cross check, so it can fight in the Assault.

This T-72 does not need to make a Cross Check as it is able to get around the side of the obstacle to contact the enemy team.

DEFENSIVE FIRE

The Motor Rifle Company shoots at the M1 Abrams as they Charge into Contact. Each team shoots at a tank within 8"/20cm using their Halted ROF.

One T-72 is within 8"/20cm of the Assaulting tanks, so it can shoot in Defensive Fire, the other one cannot.

Defensive Fire always hits Side armour, so the infantry's RPG-7 anti-tank weapons can stop the M1 Abrams despite their thick armour.

2) OPPONENT'S DEFENSIVE FIRE

After the Assaulting Unit Charges into Contact, the opposing player conducts their Defensive Fire as the Assaulting Teams close into contact with them.

Each enemy Team within 8"/20cm of an Assaulting Team (one that is in Contact with an enemy Team) is a Defending Team and Shoots as if it was their Shooting Step.

Defending Teams shoot at their Halted ROF unless they are Pinned Down, in which case they shoot at their Moving ROF. Defending Teams must target an Assaulting Team within 8"/20cm, and can only allocate hits to Assaulting Teams within 8"/20cm.

Defending Teams cannot fire Artillery Bombardments as Defensive Fire.

As they are stationary, Defending Infantry Teams do not block Line of Sight for Defensive Fire.

NO MISTAKEN TARGET

In an Assault the enemy is too close to mistake, so the Assaulting player cannot use the Mistaken Target rule.

CLOSING WITH THE ENEMY

If an Infantry Team was in Contact with the enemy through a friendly Infantry Team that is Destroyed, the Team immediately occupies its place, remaining in Contact with the enemy.

SNEAKING UP ON TANKS

A Tank Team cannot conduct Defensive Fire (although other Tank Teams in the Unit may) if any Assaulting Infantry Team that is in Contact with it:

- did not Move in the Movement Step,
- did not use any Movement Orders,
- did not Shoot in the Shooting step, and
- started its Charge into Contact Concealed by Short or Tall terrain.

SNEAKING UP ON TANKS

The Mech Platoon are assaulting some T-72 tanks. Because they are Concealed within 4"/10cm and did not move or shoot this turn, the M249 SAW teams can sneak up on the tanks.

The remaining T-72 tank can still shoot in Defensive Fire.

The M249 SAW teams Charged into Contact with two T-72 tanks. These tanks cannot shoot in Defensive Fire.

FORCING THE ASSAULT TO FALL BACK

A US M113 Mech platoon launched as Assault against a Soviet Motor Rifle Company. Unfortunately the Soviets manage to score five hits in Defensive Fire.

The M113 Mech Platoon is Pinned Down and the Assaulting Teams must Fall Back until they are more than 2"/5cm from the Defending Teams.

DEFENSIVE FIRE HITS SIDE ARMOUR
Tanks use their Side armour rating for any Armour Saves against Defensive Fire, even when the front of the vehicle is facing the shooting Team.

NO BULLETPROOF COVER
Assaulting Teams are never in Bulletproof Cover from Defensive Fire, but may be Concealed.

FORCING THE ASSAULT TO FALL BACK
A Unit that takes at least five hits from Defensive Fire becomes Pinned Down and its Teams Fall Back the shortest distance necessary until its Teams are more than 2"/5cm from the enemy, and the Assault is over. A larger Unit with at least twelve Assaulting Teams needs to take at least eight hits to become Pinned Down and Fall Back.

If all of the Assaulting Teams are Armoured Tank Teams, they only Fall Back if two of more of them (or all of them if fewer), are Bailed Out or Destroyed by Defensive Fire, regardless of the number of hits they take. When a Unit Falls Back, any Tanks that were Bailed Out by the Defensive Fire also Fall Back to reflect being hit while closing to contact.

3) ROLL TO HIT
If the Assaulting Unit was not forced to Fall Back by Defensive Fire (and still has Teams in Contact with the enemy), roll one die for each Team in Contact with the enemy. The score To Hit is the Assault rating on the Assaulting Team's Unit Card.

If the score is greater than or equal to the Assaulting Team's rating, they have scored a hit on the Team they are in Contact with. If they are in Contact with several Teams, the Defending player chooses which one is hit. Since Tanks cannot Assault Tanks, a hit from a Tank cannot be assigned to another Tank.

A Unit hit in an Assault is immediately Pinned Down.

ROLL TO HIT

One T-72 rolls a five, destroying the Infantry team it is in contact with. The other T-72 rolls a two, so the enemy teams survives.

COURAGE 4+	SKILL 5+
MORALE 3+	ASSAULT 5+
REMOUNT 3+	COUNTERATTACK 4+

Each T-72 tank rolls a die to hit, comparing it against their Assault number.

HIT TOP OR SIDE ARMOUR

An RPG-7 team scores a hit on an M60 tank. The player can choose to use the RPG-7's Anti-tank rating of 17 against the tank's side armour, or use grenades to have Anti-tank 2 against its Top armour.

WEAPON	RANGE	ROF HALTED	ROF MOVING	ANTI-TANK	FIRE-POWER	
AK-74 assault rifle team or RPG-18 anti-tank	8"/20CM	3	3	1	5+	Pinned ROF 1
	8"/20CM	1	1	14	5+	HEAT, Slow Fir
RPG-7 anti-tank team	12"/30CM	1	1	17	4+	Assault 6, HEA
PKM LMG team	16"/40CM	7	4	2	6	Assault 6, Hea

They choose to use the RPG-7's Anti-tank rating, so the M60 will make an Armour Save using its Side armour of 8.

4) ROLL SAVES

The target player rolls Saves for each hit.

HIT TOP OR SIDE ARMOUR

When a hit is scored on an Armoured Tank Team, the Assaulting Team has two options:

- It can use the Anti-tank rating of one of its normal weapons against the Tank's Side armour rating (as long as the Tank is in its Field of Fire and the weapon does not have a Minimum range).
- It can use hand grenades and other improvised anti-tank weapons, giving it an Anti-tank rating of 2 and Firepower 1+ against the Tank's Top armour.

ROLL SAVES FOR ARMOURED TANKS

The targeted player rolls a save for each hit on an Armoured Tank Team in the same way as hits from Shooting are saved (see pages 46 and 47) with the same consequences for failed Saves.

NO SAVES IF NOT ARMOURED

Infantry and Unarmoured Tank Teams hit in an Assault are automatically Destroyed. If a Transport Team is Destroyed, all of its Passengers are also Destroyed.

5) CHECK IF THE ASSAULT IS OVER

The Assaulting Unit has won if all Defending Teams that could be Contacted by the Assaulting Teams with a further 4"/10cm Move have been Destroyed or are Bailed Out. If the Assaulting Unit has won, the Defending Teams must now Break Off (see page 63).

HAS THE ASSAULTING UNIT WON

Since there are no defending Infantry teams within 4"/10cm of the Assaulting T-72 tanks, the Soviets win the Assault.

Tanks can't assault tanks, so the M113 personnel carrier does not stop the Soviets winning the Assault.

6) TEST TO COUNTERATTACK

If the Assaulting Unit did not win the Assault, the opponent rolls a single die and compares it with the Counterattack rating of each Defending Unit in turn.

- If the score is greater than or equal to the Unit's Counterattack rating, that Unit may Counterattack or Break Off as the player chooses.
- Otherwise, that Unit must Break Off.

COMMANDER'S LEADERSHIP

If one or more Units failed to Counterattack, re-roll the die and apply the new result to Units that failed to Counterattack and whose Commander is within 6"/15cm and in Line of Sight of the Unit Leader (including the Commander's own HQ Unit).

7) COUNTERATTACK...

When the defender Counterattacks, all Teams from the Assaulting Unit become Defending Teams, and vice versa.

The Assaulting Teams (previously Defending Teams) that are not in Contact with a Defending Team can Charge into Contact with a Defending Team (even if Pinned Down). Even if a Tank Team doesn't move, it must still roll to Cross any Difficult Terrain between it and the Defending Team.

Any Teams that can't Contact an enemy Defending Team do not Assault.

The counterattacking player then continues with the Assault in the same manner as the original Assaulting player, except that there is no Defensive Fire against a Counterattack.

If the counterattacking teams do not win the Assault, the original Assaulting player then Tests to Counterattack. The assault continues back and forth like this until one side or the other wins.

COUNTERATTACK

The T-72 Tank Unit Counterattacks and Charges into Contact.

The tanks that are not in Contact move into Contact with a Defending US infantry team.

A Counterattack follows all the rules for charging into contact. Fortunately the fence does not require a Cross check.

...OR BREAK OFF

A Unit that Breaks Off is Pinned Down. All Teams from the Unit immediately Move at Tactical speed the shortest distance needed to be further than 6"/15cm away from all Assaulting Teams. If the Team cannot Move more than 6"/15cm from all Assaulting Teams (or fails a roll to Cross terrain while attempting to do so), it immediately surrenders and is Destroyed.

Once a Unit has Broken Off, it is no longer a Defending Unit. If all Defending Units Break Off, the Assaulting Unit automatically Wins the Assault and can Consolidate.

CONSOLIDATING

The victorious Unit may now Move up to 4"/10cm in any direction, but cannot Charge into Contact. This Move may not bring them within 2"/5cm of an enemy Team.

If the Move takes a Team back to a Foxhole occupied by one of its Unit's Teams at the start of the Assault, it may reoccupy it. Any remaining unoccupied Foxholes are removed.

BREAK OFF

The Motor Rifle Company chooses to Break Off from the assault.

Each team moves at Dash speed until it is more than 4"/10cm away from the assaulting infantry.

If they could not get 4"/10cm away from the assaulting infantry they would surrender.

UNIT MORALE

For the price of two dead and six wounded, Team Yankee had held. But the Team had reached the end of its rope. Even as they stood there, Bannon could tell that the stress and strain of this last fight had used up every man's final reserve of energy. They had done their best and done well. But there was no more to give. Besides the exhaustion, the tanks were down to a grand total of thirty-one main gun rounds and four thousand rounds for the COAX and loader's machine gun. Even if the men could hold up under another attack, which was impossible, the ammunition couldn't. Now the Team's mission was to save what was left for another day.

IN GOOD SPIRITS

A Unit is In Good Spirits if:
- it does not have any Teams Bailed Out or Destroyed,

or
- it still has at least:
  - two Tank Teams that are not Bailed Out.
  - three Infantry Teams, or
  - one Aircraft Team.

Only count Teams that are In Command (page 31). If the Unit Leader has been Destroyed and not replaced, the unit is not In Good Spirits.

UNIT MORALE TEST

A Unit that is *not* In Good Spirits needs to take a Morale Test at the start of the player's turn after testing to Remount Bailed Out tanks.

When a Unit takes a Morale Test, roll a die:
- If the score is greater than or equal to the Unit's Morale rating, the Unit fights on.
- Otherwise, the Unit is Destroyed.

DESTROYED UNITS

When a Unit is Destroyed, all Destroyed and Bailed Out Armoured Tank Teams remain in place as Wrecks (page 49), while all remaining Teams are removed.

If a Transport Unit fails its Morale Test, its Passengers are Pinned Down and Dismount before the Unit is removed.

COMMANDER'S LEADERSHIP

Re-roll all failed Morale Tests for Units whose Commander is within 6"/15cm and in Line of Sight of the Unit Leader.

COMMANDERS ALWAYS STAND AND FIGHT

Being heroic, HQ Units never have to take a Unit Morale Test.

ATTACHMENTS

A Unit that has an Attached Unit (page 19) treats the Attached Unit as a separate Unit for Unit Morale Tests. However, if an Infantry Unit is Destroyed or fails its Morale Test, its Transport Attachment is removed from the game, but is not Destroyed.

Other types of Attached Units, such as an Infantry Attachment to a Tank Unit, continue to fight if their core Unit is Destroyed.

A Soviet Tank Company of four T-72 tanks has one tank destroyed and two Bailed Out. Having failed to remount either of the two Bailed out T-72 tanks, it does not have the the required two tanks still active, so is not In Good Spirits and needs to take a Unit Morale Test. If it fails, the crews of the Bailted Out tanks will Destroy their tanks and flee the battlefield with the surviving tank.

FORMATION MORALE

Bannon informed the brigade commander that the battalion was no longer capable of continuing the attack. Bannon ran down a list of the reasons why and waited for an answer. When he finished, there was a moment of silence on the brigade net while the grim news sank in. Then, without hesitation or a long-winded discussion, Colonel Brunn contacted the commander of the 1st of the 4th Armor and ordered him to pass through the mech battalion and continue the attack north as the brigade's lead element. Brunn came back to Bannon, ordering him to rally the battalion and to keep the brigade S-3 posted on its status. For the moment, Task Force 1st of the 78th Infantry was out of the war.

IN GOOD SPIRITS

A Formation is In Good Spirits if it has at least two Units (including the HQ Unit, but not any Transport Units) from the Formation on the table or in Reserves (page 78). Remember, Support Units are not part of any Formation, so will not keep them In Good Spirits.

FORMATION MORALE

A Formation that is *not* In Good Spirits at the start of a turn, after taking any required Morale tests, is automatically Destroyed and all of its remaining Units are Destroyed (page 64).

NO FORMATIONS LEFT

If a player has no Formations In Good Spirits (other than Allied Formations), they lose the game and their opponent takes all Objectives (page 76).

The US M1 Abrams Armored Combat Team has suffered severe casualties with just the HQ Unit of M1 Abrams tanks and the supporting M109 Field Artillery Battery still on table in Good Spirits, and nothing in reserve.

Since Support Units don't count, it doesn't have the required two Units on table in Good Spirits, so is Destroyed.

WEAPON SPECIAL RULES

Rapid-fire tank cannon coupled with a computerized fire control and laser range finders were capable of firing up to eight aimed rounds per minute at tank-sized targets at ranges in excess of 2000 meters. Guided munitions, fired from ground launchers or helicopters, had a better than ninety percent probability of hitting a target at 4000 meters. Soviet multiple rocket launchers could fire hundreds of rockets in a single volley and destroy everything within a one-by-one kilometer grid. All the implements of war had become more capable, more deadly. In all the armies arrayed across the continent, the only thing that technology had not improved was the ability of the human body to absorb punishment.

Some weapons have features or technology that make them more effective. These special rules reflect this.

AA MG

Machine-guns need high-angle mountings and rapid traverse to track fast-moving aircraft.

AA MG weapons can Shoot at Aircraft with a ROF of 1 (see page 39).

ACCURATE

Weapons with advanced range finders or sights are very accurate at long range, but need time to use properly.

Accurate weapons do not suffer the usual +1 to hit penalty if the targeted Team is more than 16"/40cm away and the Shooting Team did not Move.

ADVANCED STABILISERS

Modern three-axis stabilisers allow tanks to fire accurately on the move over almost any terrain.

A Team using weapons fitted with an Advanced Stabiliser has a higher Tactical speed. Only stabilised weapons can Shoot, and the Team cannot Assault, if the Team moves more than 10"/25cm.

ANTI-HELICOPTER

Some automatic cannons, while unsuitable for attacking other types of aircraft, can engage helicopters.

Anti-Helicopter weapons can shoot at Helicopters with a ROF of 1 (see page 39).

BRUTAL

Large-calibre guns pack enough explosive to destroy any unprotected target outright.

Infantry and Unarmoured Tank Teams re-roll successful Saves against Brutal Weapons.

DEDICATED AA

Units tasked with air defence constantly scan the skies. They react quickly and lethally whenever enemy aircraft appear.

Dedicated AA weapons use their normal ROF (rather than ROF 1) when firing at Aircraft.

FORWARD FIRING

Hull-mounted weapons and most towed guns cannot traverse to track targets to the side of the weapon.

Forward-firing weapons can only target Teams fully in front of the shooting Team, and can only fire an Artillery Bombardment if the Aiming Point is fully in front of the shooting Team.

GUIDED

The Missile Age heralded weapons that could be guided on to the target giving a high probability of hitting targets at any range. They are expensive though, so aren't wasted on targets better handled by other weapons.

Guided weapons do not suffer the usual +1 to hit penalty if the targeted Team is more than 16"/40cm away. Guided weapons cannot hit Infantry Teams unless the Infantry are stationary and in Bulletproof Cover.

GUIDED AA

Anti-aircraft missiles are specialised for shooting down strike aircraft and helicopters, making them useless against ground targets.

Guided AA weapons are Guided weapons that cannot target Tank or Infantry Teams. Guided AA weapons use their normal ROF (rather than ROF 1) when firing at Aircraft.

HEAT

When a High Explosive Anti-Tank (HEAT) warhead explodes it forms a jet of metal that can punch through a tank's armour. Since it doesn't rely on velocity, it is equally effective at any range.

The target Team's Armour rating is not increased if the targeted Team is more than 16"/40cm away when hit by HEAT weapons, but these weapons are also affected by Bazooka Skirts, BDD, Chobham, and ERA armour (see page 46).

LASER RANGEFINDER

High-tech laser rangefinders significantly improve the chance of a long-range hit.

Weapons equipped with Laser Rangefinders do not suffer the usual +1 to hit penalty if the targeted Team is more than 16"/40cm away, whether the Team Moved or not.

ONE SHOT

Some weapons systems are one-shot weapons. Once they are fired, that's it for the battle.

One Shot weapons can only fire once per game.

OVERHEAD FIRE

Light mortars sit back firing over the heads of the advancing troops to knock out enemy machine-gun nests.

Grenade launchers and light mortars capable of Overhead Fire can fire over friendly teams.

PINNED ROF 1

Submachine-gun and assault rifle-type weapons are very effective on the move, but lose their effectiveness when Pinned Down.

These weapons have a ROF of 1 when Pinned Down.

RADAR

Anti-aircraft radars make tracking fast-moving aircraft much easier, especially at long range.

Weapons equipped with Radar increase their Range by +12"/30cm and do not suffer the usual +1 penalty To Hit for range over 16"/40cm when Shooting at Aircraft.

RECOILLESS

Recoilless weapons are light enough to be carried by their crew or mounted on a jeep. The downside is the huge backblast that makes them easy to spot.

A Team firing a Recoilless weapon cannot be Concealed if it shot in its previous Shooting Step.

SLOW FIRING

Large calibre guns are slow to reload at the best of times, severely limiting their ability to hit anything while moving.

Slow-firing weapons add +1 to the score needed To Hit when moving.

STABILISER

Stabilisers keep the gun on target while moving across country. They are not perfect, especially at high speed, but they make fighting on the move possible.

A Team using weapons fitted with Stabilisers may increase its Tactical speed to 14"/35cm, but increases the score needed To Hit by +1 if it does so. Only stabilised weapons can Shoot and the Team cannot Assault if the Team moves more than 10"/25cm.

SMOKE

Blowing the enemy up is always a good option, but sometimes blinding them is better.

Smoke weapons can Shoot Smoke ammunition (see page 50).

SMOKE BOMBARDMENT

Artillery delivered smoke screens allow you to cover the flank of your advance or blind the enemy defences as you advance.

Smoke Bombardment weapons can fire a Smoke Bombardment once per game (see page 56).

EQUIPMENT SPECIAL RULES

Because of the range and the quality of the image produced on the thermal sight, it was difficult, at first, to distinguish which of the attacking blobs were tanks and which were BMPs. Bannon therefore ordered the 2nd Platoon to engage the lead vehicles with SABOT, assuming that the Soviets would follow their own tactical doctrine and lead off with tanks. The 3rd Platoon was to fire over the village at the center and rear of the attacking formation as it came out from the tree line. They would engage with HEAT on the assumption that the BMPs would be following the tanks.

Soldiers carry and tanks are fitted with various items of equipment. These special rules tell you how these affect the game.

AMPHIBIOUS

Many light tanks can swim, slowly, if needed, allowing them to cross rivers without the need for a bridge.

Amphibious Teams treat Impassable Water as Difficult Going.

BAZOOKA SKIRTS

After seeing the effectiveness of German 'bazookas' in the Second World War, the British fitted their post-war battle tanks with 'bazooka skirts', spaced armour to protect them from light, hand-held anti-tank weapons.

Teams with Bazooka Skirts have a Front and Side armour rating of 10 (unless already higher) against HEAT weapons.

BDD ARMOUR

Starting with late models of the T-72, Soviet tanks were built with layered armour, particularly on the turret front. Nicknamed 'Dolly Parton' for their twin bulges, these tanks are well protected, especially against HEAT warheads.

Teams with BDD Armour have a Side Armour rating of 13 against HEAT weapons.

CHOBHAM ARMOUR

Chobham is a high-tech armour that is very effective at stopping anti-tank rounds, particularly HEAT warheads.

Teams with Chobham Armour have a Side Armour rating of 16 against HEAT weapons.

DRAGON MOUNT

The M113 personnel carrier has a mounting for the M47 Dragon missile beside its .50 cal machine-gun.

M47 Dragon missile teams may fire while Mounted as a Passenger in a M113 Transport, using the Passenger Fired M47 Dragon missile weapons line.

ERA ARMOUR

Explosive Reactive Armour (ERA) covers a tank in slabs of explosive covered in metal plates. When an anti-tank round hits it, the ERA explodes, disrupting the round and reducing its effect. ERA armour works best against HEAT ammunition.

Teams with ERA Armour have a Side Armour rating of 16 against HEAT weapons.

HAMMERHEAD

The M901 Improved Tow Vehicle mounts its armament in a 'hammerhead' turret, allowing it to remain concealed behind cover while shooting.

A Team with a Hammerhead can remain Gone to Ground while shooting its missiles.

HEAVY WEAPON

The infantry contains a mix of rifle teams and support weapons teams. These heavy weapons are not very mobile.

A Heavy Weapon Team cannot Charge into Contact, but may be an Assaulting Team if in Contact with an enemy Team.

INFRA-RED

Infra-red night-vision equipment makes it much easier to locate targets at night.

A Unit with an Infra-red rolls two dice on the Night Visibility Table and chooses the highest score (see page 84).

MINE CLEARING DEVICES

Mine ploughs, rollers, and flails allow tanks to clear minefields (see page 85).

PASSENGERS

Armoured personnel carriers have space to carry troops inside.

A Transport Team can carry Infantry Teams as Passengers. The # indicates how many Teams can be carried.

THERMAL IMAGING

Thermal-imaging sights give a gunner a huge advantage in identifying and hitting a target at night.

A Unit using Thermal Imaging rolls two dice on the Night Visibility Table (see page 84) and chooses the highest score. In addition, Teams using Thermal Imaging do not suffer the +1 to hit penalties for Night and Smoke (see pages 44, 50, and 56).

UNARMOURED

While mounting a gun on a truck or half-track gives it mobility, it's still not a tank and can't assault.

An Unarmoured Tank team cannot Charge into Contact and must Break Off if Assaulted.

SPECIAL ABILITIES

Second Lt. Rodney Unger was a good FIST Team chief. He still had a lot to learn about tanks and infantry. But he knew about artillery and how to get it. While Unger worked up his initial fire plan based on what he had been given in the first sergeant's track, Bannon started to go over the scheme of maneuver in more detail. Once Bannon finished, Unger superimposed his supporting fire plan over the scheme of maneuver. Satisfied with the soundness of the plan, he climbed out of the FIST track and returned to 66 while Unger rumbled off into the night to pass his plan on to the battalion FSE. The high-pitched whine of the FIST's modified M-113 faded into the night and was replaced by a stillness punctured at random intervals by distant artillery fire.

ASSAULT

Small weapons teams and those carrying heavy weapons are not as deadly in assault combat as specialist rifle teams.

Teams with the Assault # special rule use this number for To Hit rolls in Assaults rather than the normal one shown on the card.

HQ TRANSPORT

A Formation Commander has his own transport so he can move between units when required.

A Formation HQ Transport Team remains part of HQ Unit.

HELICOPTER

Helicopters keep low and weave in and out of terrain, often making them hard to hit by none specialised anti-aircraft troops.

Infantry Teams (other than Heavy Weapons) and AA MG weapons must re-roll successful Firepower tests when shooting at Helicopter Teams.

HUNTER-KILLER

Western helicopters use hunter-killer tactics to tackle enemy tanks. The helicopters fly extremely low, often below tree-top height to avoid detection. Once in position, they pop up over the terrain, locate their target and fire their missiles. Once the missile hits, they duck back down again, ready to repeat the exercise.

Hunter-killer Helicopters can use terrain for Concealment (see pages 41 to 42), and are Gone to Ground unless they Shoot (see page 44).

INDEPENDENT

The specialists of Independent Teams are valuable and are protected by those around them.

An Independent Team can use the Mistaken Target rule (see page 45) to reassign hits to nearby Units, but cannot Charge into Contact (see page 57), nor take an Objective (see page 76).

OBSERVER

Artillery observers have extra radios and other specialist equipment to allow them to call in artillery fire quickly and accurately.

An Observer Team can Spot for any friendly Artillery Unit (see page 51). An Observer Team reduces the score required to Range In by -1.

SCOUT

Scouts are there to keep track of the enemy, not to get into a fight. The best way to do this is 'sneak and peek'.

Scouts are Gone to Ground unless they Shoot or Assault (see page 44).

SPEARHEAD

The spearhead travels ahead of the main force during advances and screens retreats. This allows the combat elements to move quickly into position, secure in the knowledge that they will not bump into unexpected enemy units.

When a Spearhead Unit is placed on table during Deployment (but not if it arrives from Reserves or is placed outside the normal Deployment Area using this rule), the player may immediately Move its Teams at Tactical or Dash speed.

This movement may not use any Movement Orders, and may not take a Team within:

- 16"/40cm of an enemy Team it is not Concealed from,
- 8"/20cm of any enemy Team,
- 16"/40cm of the enemy Deployment Area or any Objective outside your own Deployment Area.

When Deploying their remaining Units, a player may treat the area entirely within 8"/20cm of a Spearhead Team that is In Command as an extension of their Deployment Area. Teams placed here may not be placed in the areas that a Spearhead Team may not move into.

STRIKE AIRCRAFT

The air force has many tasks across the breadth and depth of the enemy forces. Your battle is just one small part of the big picture to them, so the aircraft supporting you will often be called away to more urgent tasks.

At the start of each of their turns, the owning player may roll a die. On a score of 4+, the Strike Aircraft Unit arrives and will be placed anywhere on table in the Movement Step as long as the Aircraft stand can be placed flat on the table or suitable terrain.

If the Strike Aircraft Unit is held in Reserve (see page 78), do not start rolling until the Unit arrives from Reserve.

Aircraft shoot or bombard as normal in the Shooting Step. Just before an Aircraft attacks, the enemy can shoot their Anti-aircraft weapons at it (see page 39).

Infantry Teams (other than Heavy Weapons) and AA MG weapons must re-roll successful Firepower tests when shooting at Strike Aircraft Teams.

All Strike Aircraft are removed from the table at the end of the Shooting Step. Any casualties they suffer carry over when the Unit returns to the table.

AMERICAN

Sergeant Billy Burns peered from his M113 commander's cupola into the distance at the fence that divided Germany in two. For the past two days he'd watched the occasional head of an East German soldier, in their distinctive helmet, bob up from the dip across the border. Yesterday he'd called in a scout helicopter for a quick fly by to see what they were doing. They were clearing mines.

Today there were no heads, and this troubled Billy. As he considered dismounting and getting a little closer, there was a roar of engines from the other side of the border, followed quickly by tanks bursting through the chain link fence.

In 1985, the US Armed Forces are a proud, strong fighting force. Its soldiers are all well-trained volunteers equipped with the best weapons that modern technology can create. They are trained and equipped to fight in all weathers, by day and by night. Every US soldier knows that they are all that stands between the Communist hordes and the freedom of the Western democracies.

The United States has the most powerful armed forces in the world. Three army corps stand ready to defend Western Europe from the red horde poised across the Iron Curtain. Armoured troops' powerful M60 Patton tanks or state of the art M1, IPM1 or M1A1 Abrams tanks, mechanized infantry mounted in reliable M113 personnel carriers or new M2 Bradley infantry fighting vehicles, and light infantry of the 82nd Airborne all stand ready to stop the red tide. Cavalry and scouts deploy forward in tanks, APCs and HMMWV vehicles to thwart the enemy's progress, while anti-aircraft troops with gun and missile vehicles watch the skies.

The US Marine Corps' amphibious troops are ready to be deployed where needed with their own tanks, Light Armored Vehicles, and hard fighting infantry, backed by their own support. Those commies won't know what hit them!

With superior weapons like the Cobra and Apache helicopter gunships, and the A-10 Warthog, America's first purpose-built close support aircraft, giving them every chance of victory. Though outnumbered, they must use every ounce of skill and cunning they possess to overcome all obstacles.

SOVIET

Rays of dawn light pierced through the gaps in the forest canopy as Yuri Volkov waited in his command tank. Soon his battalion of T-64 tanks would spring from their positions camouflaged amongst the trees and join the rest of the regiment as they storm across the West German frontier.

The war Yuri had been training his men for had arrived, and though he had little doubt of the savage fighting to come, he was supremely confident in his men and their equipment.

He signalled the advance and his T-64 tanks rolled forward. A flash in the distance marked the first response of the enemy and his tankers began to return fire.

Faced with the destruction of the Socialist Workers' Paradise, it is the duty of every Soviet citizen to commit their lives to the struggle against the Capitalist exploiters and to free the workers of Europe. The Soviet Army is a true citizen army, with every adult male trained in the latest scientific combat techniques, and the might of Soviet industry has created modern weapons in numbers sufficient to arm the population for the coming struggle.

The Soviet science of war requires that the strength of the army be concentrated at critical points to overwhelm the enemy with superior firepower, then the subsequent victory exploited with utmost speed and ruthlessness. Short-term casualties must be traded for long-term victory.

The Soviet Union's most powerful forces are stationed in East Germany and Czechoslovakia, poised on the border with West Germany ready to strike at a moment's notice. They are equipped with the very best Soviet industry has to offer, from sophisticated missile firing T-80 and T-64 tanks, and powerful T-72 tanks to versatile BMP infantry fighting vehicles, as well as plentiful BTR-60 armoured personnel carriers. Supported by elite Afgansty Air Assault troops, powerful self-propelled artillery, and effective and numerous anti-tank and anti-aircraft weapons, there will be little that the corrupt capitalist armies of NATO can do to stop them. Soon the western workers will be free and the dawn of a new socialist age will begin!

BRITISH

'All Call Signs Charlie, Zero Bravo', Major Charles Leslie alerted his troops. 'Move in five.'

C Squadron, 17th/21st Lancers, and the Irish Guardsmen supporting them made their last-minute preparations, each man checking his weapons one more time and going through the little rituals that had become talismans against violent death.

After days of hard fighting, they were worn and frayed, no longer so eager to test themselves in battle. Their expressions were grim and hard. The coming battle was not going to be easy. The Soviets fought tenaciously to hold what they'd taken. It wouldn't matter though. C Squadron would live up to the regimental motto: 'Death or Glory', and today it would be the enemy that would die and C Squadron that would reach for glory.

When World War III broke out in August 1985, the British Army Of the Rhine (BAOR) had been defending the West on the border between West Germany and East Germany for just over forty years. These soldiers, the third generation of British soldiers to stand watch on the North German Plain, quickly proved their mettle.

With its usual professionalism, the British Army had prepared for war. Now, as the Soviet Army flooded across the border into West Germany, it was ready and waiting. Scorpion and Scimitar light tanks skirmished with the Soviet forward detachments as the Chieftain and Challenger armoured regiments waited. The infantry held the towns and woods, forcing the enemy into killing zones. If anything broke through, the airmobile troops in their Lynx helicopters would hold them. The British Army is ready.

WEST GERMAN

Hauptmann Müller watched from his turret as the Soviet T-72s emerged from the village.

'Wait' he thought to himself as more enemy tanks moved beyond the cover of the village houses. The Soviet tanks keep coming, he counted eight, no nine, but more kept coming. They spread out slowly into line abreast, unaware that Müller's company of Leopard 2 tanks were watching them from the forest just 1500 metres away.

Müller could wait no longer.

"FIRE," he ordered and the world around the Soviet tanks erupted in flame and destruction...

The West German *Bundeswehr* (Armed Forces) is a force of well-motivated national service conscripts lead a by highly skilled body of professional officers and non-commisioned officers.

All across West Germany divisions are being mobilised and reservists flock to their barracks for assignment to the front. In the sector of the cities of Hannover and Braunschweig the men of *1. Panzerdivision* stand ready to face the Soviet hordes as they pour across the border from East Germany.

The West Germans have powerful Leopard 2 tanks and panzergrenadiers mounted in the Marder infantry fighting vehicles in their panzer brigades, backed up by self-propelled artillery, armoured cars, and missile armed tank-hunters. Their panzergrenadier brigades are are also well-equipped with Leopard 1 tanks, more panzergrenadier in Marders and M113s. In the skies Tornado strike aricraft roar in at low level to strikes the enemy with speed and precission, while Bo-105 PAH anti-tank helicopters lurk low to the ground and behind forests to pop up and knock out the enemy tanks when they least expect it.

These troops fight with skill and cunning to slow the Soviet advance, determined to protect their homes and families.

WARSAW PACT

At the end of the World War II in 1945, the world breathed a sigh of relief. However, the face of Europe had changed dramatically. A new global political divide had been formed between the Communist East and Democratic West. The West formed the North Atlantic Treaty Organisation (NATO) in 1949, and in response the Warsaw Pact was formed by the Soviet Union and its allies, including East Germany, Poland, and Czechoslovakia, in 1955.

EAST GERMANY

The East German *Volksarmee*, or Peoples' Army, has the reputation of being the most well-trained of all the Warsaw Pact armies. It has a high proportion of professional soldiers and is well-equipped. *9. Panzerdivision*, or 9th Tank Division, in particular is equipped with T-72M tanks and BMP-1 and BMP-2 infantry fighting vehicles. The motor rifle divisions are equipped with fully modernised T-55AM2 tanks, BMP-1s and BTR-60 8-wheeled armoured personal carriers.

POLAND

The Polish People's Army (*Ludowe Wojsko Polskie* or LWP) are also a part of the Warsaw Pact, fighting alongside the Soviets in the fight against capitalisim. The Polish people have a reputation as a hard fighting nation throughout their long history. Poles field T-72M and T-55 tank battalions, as well as BMP tracked and wheeled wheeled motor rifle battalions.

CZECHOSLOVAKIA

The Czechoslovakian arms industry flourishes with many indigenous designs seeing service with the Czechoslovak forces as well as with Poland. The Czechoslovak People's Army field T-72M and T-55 Tank Battalions, as well as BMP and wheeled motor rifle battalions. These are backed up by unique equipment like the Dana 152mm self-propelled gun, the RM-70 multiple rocket launcher, and the OT-64 wheeled armoured personnel carrier.

NATO FORCES

Since its inception in 1949, NATO has been a community of free nations brought together with a common goal, to defend the freedom of Western Europe and North America. To do this Canada, France and the Netherlands deploy armoured and mechanised forces in West Germany. Old allies have also been called on, and an ANZAC Brigade of Australian and New Zealand troops answers the call to fight.

CANADA
Canadians field 105mm armed Leopard 1 tanks and M113 mechanised infantry. Recon options include the Lynx tracked vehicle based on the M113. Canadian support includes M109 artillery, ADATS anti-tank/anti-aircraft missile carriers, and M150 TOW armed missile vehicles.

FRANCE
France has its own 105mm armed AMX-30 tank, while infantry travel in AMX-10P IFVs or 4x4 VAB APCs. France's reconnaissance are heavily armed AMX-10 RC armoured car. The French have their own rapid fire AMX AuF1 SP 155mm howitzers, Roland surface-to-air self-propelled missile systems, and Mephisto HOT armed anti-tank guided missile vehicles.

THE NETHERLANDS
The Dutch have Leopard 1 and new Leopard 2 tanks, and mount their infantry in YPR-765 IFVs. For reconnaissance they use the M113 C&V tracked vehicle. For artillery support they use the M109 Self-propeeled howitzer, PTRL SP AA tanks for anti-aircraft work, and PRAT TOW missile vehicles.

ANZAC
Australia fields Leopard 1 tanks, and they and their ANZAC colleagues from New Zealand have M113 mounted mechanised infantry. The Australians also provide recon with turreted M113s For support the call of the troops of the British 2nd Corps.

MIDDLE EAST

With Europe ablaze the shadow of war quickly crept across the globe. In the Middle East, Iran and Iraq had been locked in a conflict across their border since 1980, and looked unlikely to stop anytime soon. Further west, Israel and Syria had come to blows in Lebanon as Israel fought PLO forces operating from inside their northern neighbour. The oil rich region, already rife with conflict and tension, was about to be drawn into World War III as the Soviet Union and US led NATO set about protecting their interests in the black gold that kept the wheels of industry turning.

ISRAEL
The Israel Defence Force had is a very experienced fighting force, having fought wars in 1967, 1973, and 1982. They are equipped with their own indiginous tank, the Merkava, as wwll as a variety of US supplied and captured Soviet equipment.

IRAQI
Iraqi has been at was with Iran since 1980 and has a massive army made up of conscripts. Their equipment is dominated by Soviet weapons supplimented by French and Chinese imports.

SYRIA
Like Iraq, Syrian forces are conscripted. Syria as a closer relationship with the Soviet union and almost all of its weapons come from Warsaw Pact sources.

IRAN
Iran's armed forces are a mix of conscripts, professionals and revolutionary inspired religious volunteers. Iran became an Islamic Republic in 1979, and thought is became an international pariah, it inheriated a mixed bag of equipment from West Germany, Britain, United States and the Soviet Union from the previous government.

PICKING YOUR FORCE

Before a game, you need to pick the Formations and Units that will make up your force. There are two ways to do this:
- build to a points limit, or
- build for a specific scenario.

POINTS LIMIT

If you are playing a pick-up game with a friend, you can agree to a points limit before the game, say 50, 75, 100, 125, or even 150 points. Then pick your force from a Force Diagram so that the total points value of all of your Units is no more than the agreed amount.

SCENARIO

You and a friend could organise a scenario game instead. Linking your scenarios into a campaign allows you to extend the story across multiple games. In a scenario, you decide on a situation that would provide an interesting challenge for both players and select two forces that fit the scenario.

The forces use in a scenario will usually be based on a Force Diagram, but may contain variations specific to the scenario. The two forces might have the same points total, or they might not, it all depends on the scenario you are creating. If one force is much stronger than the other, the scenario will usually include some additional difficulty for the stronger force to make the game fun for both players.

CHOOSING A FORCE

The first part of picking your force is to choose the Force Diagram you will use. You'll find Force diagrams in *World War III: Team Yankee* army books. Select the book covering the nationality you want and you're ready to go.

PICKING FORMATIONS

Next pick your Formations. There are seven to choose from in our Force Diagram: two Armoured Squadrons, two Mechanised Squadrons, two Recce Squadrons, and an Airmobile company. You can take any or all of these, or even multiple of the same Formation.

Your Force must contain at least one Formation, but you can field as many Formations as your points allow. Choosing Formations from a Force Diagram gives you access to Support Units, such as divisional artillery or reconnaissance units and air support from the air force, that higher command has assigned to work with your Formation.

FORMATIONS
A Force can contain as many Formations of each type as there are layers shown, but must have at least one Formation.

MULTIPLE OPTIONS
Units that are stacked indicate the number of Units of that type you can have in your Formation or Force.

SUPPORT UNITS
Units that are not part of a Formation are Support Units. You can take one of these from each box as part of your Force.

ALLIED FORMATIONS
You can take an Allied Formation to support your Force, allowing mixed NATO or mixed Warsaw Pact forces.

As support however, they won't keep fighting if your core formations run away.

INTER-DIVISIONAL SUPPORT
You may field compulsory Combat Units (with a black box) from the above Formations as Support Units.

BRITISH FORCE

ROYAL HUSSARS

CHALLENGER ARMOURED SQUADRON
TB201 — 16

STAFFORDSHIRES

WARRIOR MECHANISED COMPANY
TB203 — 19

DEATH OR GLORY BOYS
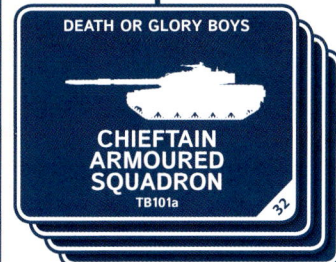
CHIEFTAIN ARMOURED SQUADRON
TB101a — 32

IRISH GUARDS

FV432 MECHANISED COMPANY
TB104a — 32

ARTILLERY
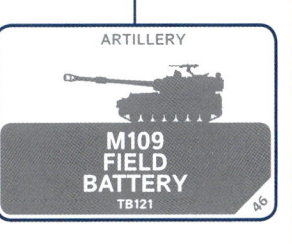
M109 FIELD BATTERY
TB121 — 46

ARTILLERY
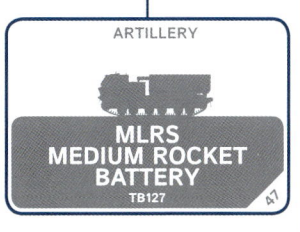
MLRS MEDIUM ROCKET BATTERY
TB127 — 47

OBSERVER

FV432 FOO
TB122a — 47

ANTI-AIRCRAFT

SPARTAN BLOWPIPE SAM SECTION
TB123 — 48

ANTI-AIRCRAFT

CHIEFTAIN MARKSMAN AA BATTERY
TB128 — 48

ANTI-AIRCRAFT

TRACKED RAPIER SAM SECTION
TB124 — 49

NATO ALLIED FORMATION
YOU MAY FIELD ONE NATO FORMATION AS AN ALLIED FORMATION
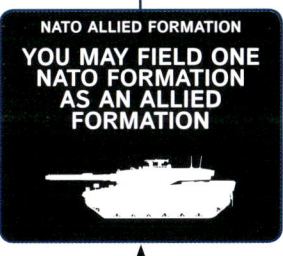

FORMATION SUPPORT
You may field compulsory Combat Units (with a black box) from the above Formations as Support Units.

AIRCRAFT
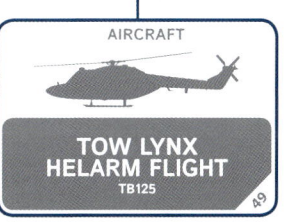
TOW LYNX HELARM FLIGHT
TB125 — 49

AIRCRAFT

TOW LYNX HELARM FLIGHT
TB125 — 49

AIRCRAFT

HARRIER CLOSE SUPPORT FLIGHT
TB126 — 49

SAMPLE CHALLANGER ARMOURED SQUADRON

For our example force over the next few pages we will be building a Challenger Armoured Formation based on the British Starter Force box.

This box contains between 88 and 100 points, depending on how you choose to build your models.

PICKING YOUR FORCE

FORMATION DIAGRAM

Formations are the core of your force and your main fighting strength. A Formation is a group of Units under a single Commander, either a NATO company or a Warsaw Pact battalion. It contains the company or battalion's own troops and their slice of their parent battalion, regiment or division's specialist weapons and units. The Formation Diagram is, in essence, a list of Unit cards that you can choose from when creating that Formation.

HQ UNIT
The HQ Unit contains the Commander, their staff, and any additional support teams. *See page 19.*

FORMATION COMMANDER
A Commander usually has the same equipment as the rest of their formation, but is braver and more skilful.

ROYAL HUSSARS
CHALLENGER ARMOURED SQUADRON

You must field the Formation HQ and one Combat Unit from each black box.
You may also field one Combat Unit from each grey box.

• TANK FORMATION • CHOBHAM ARMOUR • THERMAL IMAGING •

CHALLENGER ARMOURED SQUADRON HQ TB201

2x	Challenger	**22 POINTS**
1x	Challenger	**11 POINTS**
2x	Challenger (ROMOR)	**26 POINTS**
1x	Challenger (ROMOR)	**13 POINTS**

Challenger (ROMOR) has Front Armour 21 instead of 20, Side Armour 10 instead of 8, and Cross 3+ instead of 2+.

COURAGE 3+	SKILL 2+
MORALE 3+	ASSAULT 3+
REMOUNT 3+	COUNTERATTACK 3+

IS HIT ON 4+

	FRONT	SIDE	TOP
	20	8	2
ROMOR	21	10	2

TACTICAL	TERRAIN DASH	CROSS COUNTRY DASH	ROAD DASH	CROSS / ROMOR
10"/25CM	16"/40CM	24"/60CM	28"/70CM	2+ / 3+

WEAPON	RANGE	ROF HALTED	ROF MOVING	ANTI-TANK	FIRE-POWER	NOTES
120mm L11 gun	40"/100CM	2	1	22	2+	Brutal, Laser Rangefinder, Smoke, Stabiliser
7.62mm AA MG	16"/40CM	3	3	2	6	
7.62mm MG	16"/40CM	1	1	2	6	

ANTI-TANK

SWINGFIRE GUIDED WEAPONS TROOP TB103 — 33

WARRIOR ANTI-TANK SECTION TB212 — 20

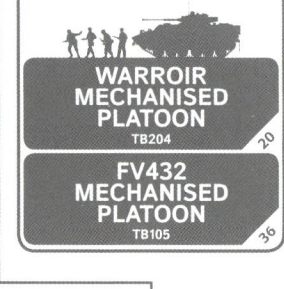

INFANTRY

WARRIOR MECHANISED PLATOON TB204 — 20

FV432 MECHANISED PLATOON TB105 — 36

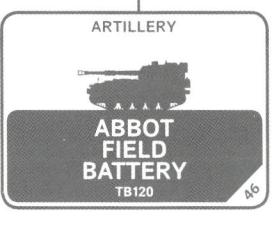

ARTILLERY

ABBOT FIELD BATTERY TB120 — 46

RECON

SCORPION RECCE TROOP TB112 — 41

You may field a Combat Unit from a black box as a Support Unit for your Force.

REQUIRED UNITS
Units shown in black are required as part of this Formation. Usually this is the HQ and two units.

OPTIONAL UNITS
Units shown in grey are optional as part of this Formation. These are mainly specialist weapons.

EITHER-OR UNITS
If a box has two or more choices in it, you may only choose one.

BUILDING A UNIT

Units are the fundamental building blocks of your force. The teams of a unit fight together as a closely-coordinated group, supporting each other as they take the fight to the enemy.

Each Unit entry or unit card tells you the possible variations of each Unit and the points cost of each configuration.

The Warrior Mechanised Platoon below has options for a full strength platoon, or a reduced strength platoon. It also has options to add extra Milan teams with their transport, as well as an option to replace their Warrior transports with Warrior (Uparmoured) transports.

WARRIOR MECHANISED PLATOON
- 4x GPMG team with 66mm anti-tank
- 3x Carl Gustav anti-tank team
- 1x 2" mortar team
- 4x Warrior [TB205] **14 POINTS**

- 3x GPMG team with 66mm anti-tank
- 2x Carl Gustav anti-tank team
- 1x 2" mortar team
- 3x Warrior [TB205] **10 POINTS**

OPTIONS
- Add two Milan missile teams & one Warrior [TB205] for +4 points.
- Replace all Warrior with Warrior (Uparmoured) [TB209] for +1 point.

SUPPORT

Looking at the Force Diagram again, there are three ways to add support: Support Units, Allied Formations and Formation Support.

SUPPORT UNITS

Support Units are things like reconnaissance and artillery that are held by the divisional commander and allocated out as needed. You can field one Unit from each box in the support area. One point to note is that while Support Units are very powerful additions to your force, they don't count towards Formation Morale tests. So if you run out of combat troops in your Formations, your Support Units will quit the field and the game is over.

ALLIED FORMATIONS

With their integrated command structures, both NATO (US, British, West German, and any other Force with a NATO Allied Formation in its support) and the Warsaw Pact (Soviet, East German, and any other Force with a Warsaw Pact Allied Formation in its support) can field formations from allied armies as part of their force.

An Allied Formation obeys all the rules for its own nationality. An Allied Formation Commander can only join Units in its own Formation (see pages 57) and only those Units benefit from its Command Leadership (see page 47, 50, and 62). As they are Support, do not count Allied Formations when determining whether you have any Formations left or if have lost the game (see page 65).

FORMATION SUPPORT

Formation Support represents a higher commander reinforcing your Formations with additional Units from other Formations. You can take any compulsory Units (other than the HQ Unit) from other Formations in your Force. You may only have one of each type of Unit as Formation Support, and only if you don't have that same type of Unit in one of your Formations already.

FORCE AND FORMATION CARDS

When picking your force, you can either use the Force Diagrams in the army books or the Force Cards. These cards have the same options as the diagrams in the books, they are just formatted as lists to fit in the smaller space. Likewise, you can use the Formation Diagrams or the Formation Cards.

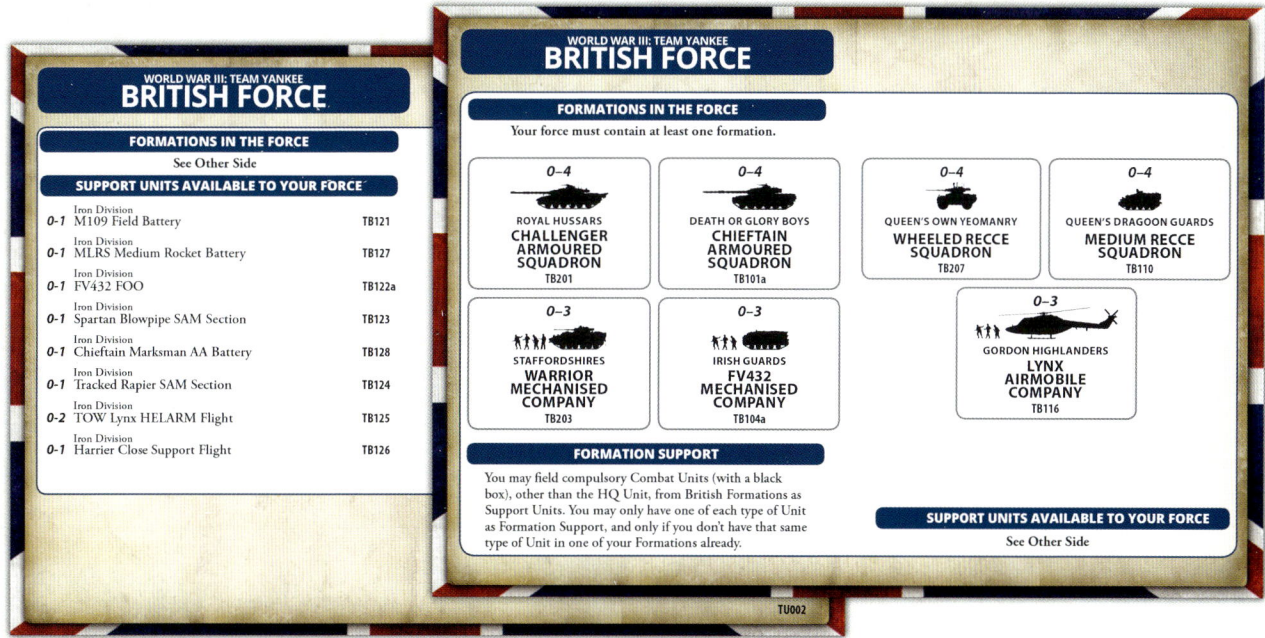

PICKING YOUR FORCE

OUR FORCE

We will take an HQ Unit of one tank, two *Challenger Armoured Troops*, and one *Warrior Anti-tank Section*. Looking at the Formation Diagram, we see that our HQ Unit's Challenger tank costs us 11 points.

Now we look at the back of the *Challenger Armoured Troop* Unit card, we see that we have a choice of two or three, Challenger or Challenger (ROMOR) tanks. Let's make one of our troops two Challenger tanks for 22 points, and the other two Challenger (ROMOR) for 26 points. We then grab the *Warrior Anti-tank Section* card and take two Warrior (Milan) for 4 points, giving a total of 63 points.

Going back to the Force Diagram, we see a variety of Support Units available to our force. Let's add a MLRS Medium Rocket Battery of two MLRS for 6 points and we'll add a TOW Lynx Helarm Flight of two helicopters for 6 points. This brings our force to 75 points.

Finally we will add some formation support from other formations. First off, for variety, we will take a Cheiftain Armoured Troop of two Cheiftains for 12 points. We are also going to add some reconnaissance, with a Scimitar Recce Troop of two Scimitars for 2 points and a Fox Recce Troop of four Foxes for 3 points. This brings our force total to 92 points.

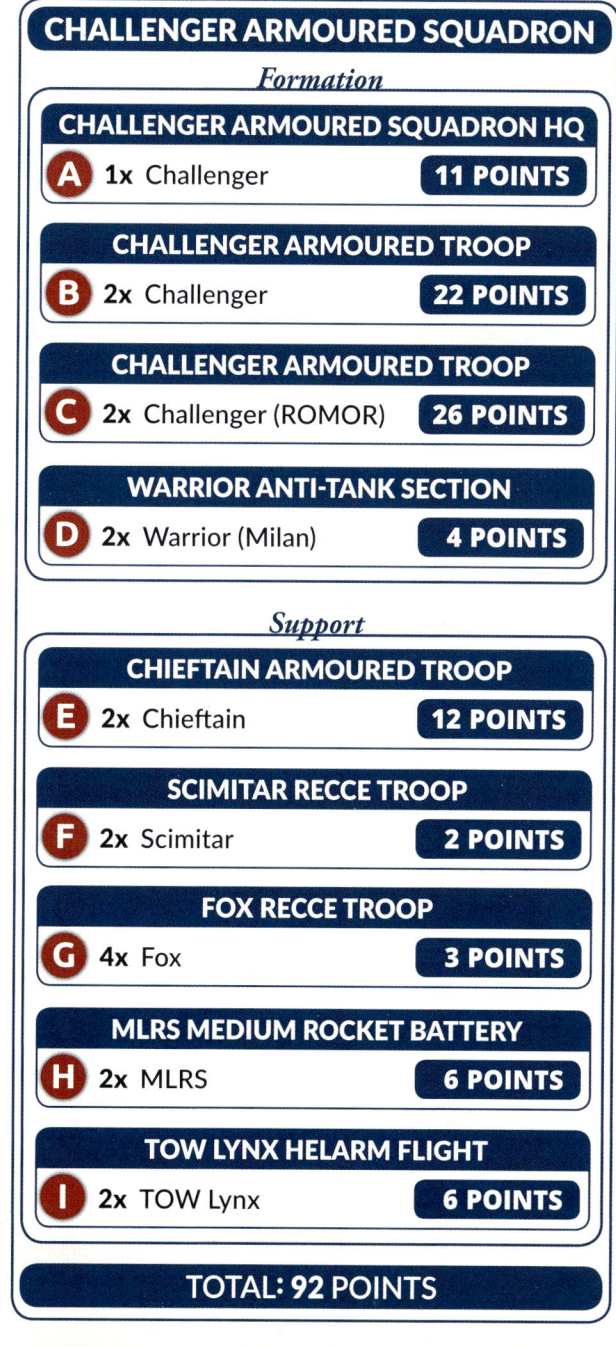

CHALLENGER ARMOURED SQUADRON

Formation

CHALLENGER ARMOURED SQUADRON HQ
- A — 1x Challenger — **11 POINTS**

CHALLENGER ARMOURED TROOP
- B — 2x Challenger — **22 POINTS**

CHALLENGER ARMOURED TROOP
- C — 2x Challenger (ROMOR) — **26 POINTS**

WARRIOR ANTI-TANK SECTION
- D — 2x Warrior (Milan) — **4 POINTS**

Support

CHIEFTAIN ARMOURED TROOP
- E — 2x Chieftain — **12 POINTS**

SCIMITAR RECCE TROOP
- F — 2x Scimitar — **2 POINTS**

FOX RECCE TROOP
- G — 4x Fox — **3 POINTS**

MLRS MEDIUM ROCKET BATTERY
- H — 2x MLRS — **6 POINTS**

TOW LYNX HELARM FLIGHT
- I — 2x TOW Lynx — **6 POINTS**

TOTAL: 92 POINTS

MISSIONS

MISSIONS

The army always has a plan, and your formation has a mission as part of that plan. While you can just stick your forces on the table and fight until one side is completely destroyed, missions and scenarios add a whole new level to the game as players struggle to take or defend specific objectives or achieve goals vital to their war effort.

SELECTING A MISSION

Your first mission should be Annihilation (see page 87) as it is a simple mission that pits one player against the other in a fight to the death. This mission is ideal for smaller forces.

Once you've played Annihilation a few times, try Free for All (page 87), which adds Objectives (page 84) to the mission to bring in new stratagems to defeat your opponent with. After that play Dust Up (page 88) to add Reserves (page 86) and a new battlefield layout to your games.

When you've got the hang of these missions, you and your opponent can either choose a mission, or one player can roll on the Random Mission Table to select one of the six easiest-to-play missions.

RANDOM MISSION TABLE	
DIE ROLL	MISSION
1	Annihilation
2	Free for All
3	Dust Up
4	Encounter
5	Counterattack
6	Contact

MORE MISSIONS

Once you've gained some experience with the first six missions, there are four more: Breakthrough, No Retreat, Rearguard, and Bridgehead for you to try. These missions introduce new twists to your battles with ambushes, minefields, and strategic withdrawals. Battle Plans (page 95) is a good way of selecting one of the full range of missions to play.

SCENARIOS

As well as playing free-form missions, you can play specific scenarios that are set up to provide interesting challenges for both players, either from our other books, our website: *www.Team-Yankee.com*, from your own imagination, or inspired by historical events in other wars. If one force is much stronger than the other, you can include some additional difficulty for the stronger force to make the game fun for both players. Linking your scenarios into a campaign extends the story across multiple games.

MORE WAYS TO PLAY

Be sure to visit the website: *www.Team-Yankee.com* for loads more exciting ways to play *Team Yankee*.

The website has downloads giving you more missions, scenarios and campaigns, along with different ways to choose the mission to play, expanded rules for fighting in the dark or at dusk, and much, much more.

You'll also find information on organising your own escalation campaigns, leagues, tournaments, and other forms of organised play, along with download packs to get you started.

On top of this, there's loads of information on the units, battles, and history of the period!

VICTORY POINTS TABLE

WINNER'S LOSSES	RESULT	WINNER'S VICTORY POINTS	LOSER'S VICTORY POINTS
0 or 1 Unit	Stunning Victory	8	1
2 Units	Major Victory	7	2
3 or more Units	Minor Victory	6	3

WHO ATTACKS

The Battle Plans (page 95) specify which player attacks, or instructs the players to roll to see who attacks. In this case, both players to roll a die. The highest-scoring player is the Attacker.

If you are not using Battle Plans, you can either roll to see who attacks (particularly suited to Meeting Engagements like Annihilation, Free for All, Encounter, and Dust Up), or have the player with more infantry formations defend. (useful for missions with a distinct attacker and defender like Hasty Attack, Counterattack, and No Retreat).

DEPLOYMENT

Each mission explains how both sides forces are deployed. Units can be held in Reserve, held in Ambush, or placed on the table.

PLACING UNITS IN COMMAND

You must place all of a Unit's Teams so that they are In Command (page 31).

ATTACHMENTS

A Transport or Infantry Unit Attachment deploys at the same time, but separately from its core Unit. They may be placed together or separately. The Passengers may be Mounted or Dismounted.

LEFT OUT OF BATTLE

At the start of the game you may elect to leave Units that you do not think will contribute, but do not want to lose, out of the battle. A Unit that is left out of battle takes no part in the game and is ignored for all purposes.

NO LEAVING THE TABLE

Once a Unit is placed on the table or arrives from Reserve, it cannot move off the table.

START IN FOXHOLES & GONE TO GROUND

All Infantry Teams start the game in Foxholes, giving them Concealment and Bulletproof Cover.

All Teams start the game Gone to Ground.

WHO HAS THE FIRST TURN

The Attacker has the first turn, except in Meeting Engagements where both players roll a die after setting up, with the higher rolling player having the first turn.

WINNING THE GAME

The goal in most missions is to take or hold Objectives. If a player has no Formations (other than Allied Formations) in Good Spirits (page 65), although they may have Support Units left, their force flees the battlefield and the enemy wins. In missions with Objectives, this leaves all of the Objectives in the hands of the enemy.

VICTORY POINTS

Refer to the Winning the Game section of the mission briefing to figure out who won. To determine the extent of the victory, count the number of Units from the Winner's Force that were Destroyed, including HQ Units, but not Independent Teams. Count core Units and their Attachments separately, so if both are Destroyed, this counts as two Units.

Look up the number of Units from the Winner's Force that were Destroyed on the Victory Points Table to see how many Victory Points each side gains.

THERE ARE NO DRAWS

Both players lose a game that runs out of time—there is no such thing as a draw in *Team Yankee*. If neither player won, both players look up the number of Surviving Units the enemy force has as though their opponent was the winner and use the Loser's Points column to determine their own Victory Points.

OBJECTIVES

Objectives are markers to indicate the importance of this point to the combatants. They are a standard large base (2½"/63mm wide by 2"/50mm deep), either marked with a symbol representing your or your opponent's army or with a small diorama modelled on it.

Objectives are not Terrain, regardless of what is modelled on the base, and do not hinder movement or provide Concealment or Bulletproof Cover, nor do they block Line of Sight.

PLACING OBJECTIVES

You must place an Objective where it will sit flat (or relatively flat) on the table or a piece of terrain where it is accessible to the enemy. You may not lean it up against a hedge or a cliff for instance, nor place it in the middle of an Impassable lake.

HOLDING OBJECTIVES

You are Holding an Objective if you start your turn with a Tank or Infantry team within 4"/10cm of an Objective, and end it with no opposing Tank or Infantry teams within 4"/10cm of that Objective.

Objectives cannot be Held by Tank Teams that are Bailed Out, Aircraft, Transports, or Independent Teams. Nor can these teams prevent the enemy from Holding an Objective.

Teams that Moved at Dash speed cannot take an Objective nor prevent the enemy from taking it.

MODELLING OBJECTIVES

While you can use a spare large base as an objective marker, it is a lot more fun to do a little modelling and stick a broken-down tank or stack of supplies on the base and create a mini diorama like this abandoned M113 below.

Alternatively, you could pick up a set of *World War III: Team Yankee* Token and Objective that are themed to your army from our website, *www.Team-Yankee.com*.

OBJECTIVES

Teams Hold an Objective if they are within 4"/10cm at the start of their turn and there are no enemy Teams within 4"/10cm of it at the end of the turn.

Bailed Out Tanks cannot take or hold Objectives.

Teams can take or hold an Objective while Pinned Down.

Objective

4"/10cm

MISSION SPECIAL RULES

Each mission has a selection of special rules that set the scene and tell you how to run the mission. Mission special rules include:

- Ambush
- Meeting Engagements
- Reserves
- Strategic Withdrawal

AMBUSH

In missions with the Ambush special rule, the ambushing player holds one or more Units (as specified in the mission) in Ambush when they deploy. Units held in Ambush are treated as being on the table, but their location isn't specified until they reveal themselves. They are held off the table at the start of the game.

ALREADY THERE

Ambushing Teams do not have to move. They can remain where they are placed and shoot at their Halted ROF.

Infantry Units are in Foxholes when they are placed on the table from Ambush.

PLACING AMBUSHES

In real life, the minor details of the terrain and small pieces of intelligence on the enemy's activities give you clues as to where they will attack, making it far easier to select the ideal place for an ambush than it is in a game. To reflect this, the ambushing player does not need to decide where their ambush will take place until it is revealed.

At the start of your turn, in the Starting Step, you may place any or all Units that you have been holding in Ambush. You must place an entire Unit at a time, and the Unit must be placed with all of its Teams In Command (page 29).

You may place a Team from Ambush anywhere in your Deployment Area (ignoring any extensions created by the Spearhead rule), provided that it is:

- at least 16"/40cm from any enemy Tank or Infantry Team within Line of Sight, unless Concealed by Terrain from it, and
- at least 4"/10cm from all enemy Tank or Infantry Teams.

ATTACHMENTS AND AMBUSHES

When you hold a Unit in Ambush, you may also hold its Transport or Infantry Attachment in Ambush as well, or Deploy them as normal. If you do hold both a Unit and its Attachment in Ambush together, the Infantry must be Mounted in their Transports when they are placed from Ambush.

PLACING AMBUSHES

Teams must be revealed more than 16"/40cm from the enemy, or more than 4"/10cm from the enemy if in Concealing Terrain or out of Line of Sight.

Teams can Ambush out of sight behind terrain, then move into sight later.

Infantry teams in the open must still be placed more than 16"/40cm from the enemy. Although they are Concealed if they remain stationary, they are not Concealed by Terrain.

Teams can never ambush within 4"/10cm of the enemy.

Teams Concealed by terrain, can Ambush if they are more than 4"/10cm away.

MEETING ENGAGEMENTS

In a Meeting Engagement (such as Free for All, Encounter, and Dust Up), players do not place their Ranged In markers as Preplanned Artillery Targets at the start of the game.

In addition, the following rules apply in the first Shooting Step of the player who has the first turn. They do not apply in the second player's turn, nor in subsequent turns.

- The first player's Strike Aircraft cannot arrive and their Helicopters must Loiter Off Table (see page 29) in their first turn.
- Treat all of the first player's Teams as having moved when Shooting in their first Shooting Step, whether they actually moved or not.
- The first player's Teams cannot fire Artillery Bombardments in their first Shooting Step.

The first player's Teams can still move or Go to Ground as normal in their Movement Step, and launch assaults in the Assault Step.

RESERVES

Some missions require you to hold part of your force in Reserve. You may not deploy more than 60% of the agreed points total for the game on the table. The remainder must be held in Reserve.

The Reserves Table helps you calculate the proportion of your force that you can deploy for a given Force size. You may deploy less and hold more in Reserve if you wish.

RESERVES	
FORCE SIZE	ON TABLE
50 points	30 points
60 points	36 points
75 points	45 points
80 points	48 points
100 points	60 points
125 points	75 points
150 points	90 points
200 points	120 points

A Unit (along with its Attachments) must be kept together. Either the whole Unit is in Reserve, or the whole Unit is deployed on table.

When a Unit arrives from Reserves, it and its Attachments Move onto the table from the table edge specified in the mission. The entire Unit must be In Command at the end of its Movement in the turn it arrives from Reserves. Attachments and their core Unit must arrive from the same point, although Passengers may be Mounted or Dismounted.

A Unit may not use Movement Orders until it has moved on to the table.

IMMEDIATE RESERVES

At the start of your first turn roll a die. On a roll of 5+ your first Unit arrives from the Reserves. It may be any Unit of your choice, but must arrive now.

At the start of your second turn roll two dice. Each roll of 5+ results in another Unit arriving from your Reserves. So, if you're lucky, you could have up to two Units arriving from Reserve during your second turn.

Keep rolling at the start of each of your following turns adding one more die than the previous turn, so at the start of turn three you roll three dice, at the start of turn four you roll four dice, and so on. Each roll of 5+ brings another Unit on from your Reserves.

If you rolled three or more dice to get Reserves in a turn, but failed to score any rolls of 5+, you automatically receive one Unit from your Reserves anyway.

DELAYED RESERVES

If the mission has Delayed Reserves, use the same rules as Immediate Reserves, except that you do not start rolling for your Reserves until turn three, and then get one die. This increases by one die per turn as normal, so that on turn four you roll two dice, on turn five you roll three dice, and so on.

DEEP RESERVES

In a mission with Deep Reserves, you may only place either one Tank Unit with front armour of 4 or more, or one Aircraft Unit on the table at the start of the game. All remaining Units of these types must be held in Reserve.

FLANKING RESERVES

In a mission with Flanking Reserves, you may have a smaller force in Reserve than usual. You must hold at least one Unit in Reserve, but may hold more in Reserve if you wish. These Reserves will arrive on the enemy flank.

SCATTERED RESERVES

When each Unit arrives from Scattered Reserve, the owning player rolls a die to determine which table edge or corner it will arrive from using the mission map as reference.

If a Unit arrives from Scattered Reserves on a table edge, it may enter the table anywhere along that table edge. If the Unit arrives from Reserves on a corner, it must enter the table within 16"/40cm of the corner.

STRATEGIC WITHDRAWAL

The Defender starts the game with no Delay Counters.

At the start of each turn from turn two onwards, after checking Formation Morale, the Defender counts the number of Units (not counting their Attachments and any Independent Teams) and Delay Counters that they have on table.

- If the total is six or more, they must Withdraw one Unit (other than an Independent Team) and its Attachments and remove all Delay Counters.
- If they have less than six Units and Delay Counters combined, they gain a Delay Counter, but do not Withdraw any Units.

WITHDRAWING UNITS

When the Defender is required to Withdraw a Unit, all of the teams of that Unit (and its Attachments) are removed from the table. If a Withdrawing Unit is not in Good Spirits, it will be treated as being Destroyed when working out Victory Points.

BASIC MISSIONS

These missions are the core missions for *Team Yankee*. As a new player you should experiment with these missions before moving on to more challenging ones.

You can also use these missions to design scenarios recreating historical battles. Pick a mission that suits the story you want to tell and tweak it to match.

ANNIHILATION

Total war means total victory or total annihilation.

SPECIAL RULES
- Meeting Engagement (Both players)

SETTING UP
The Attacker picks a long table edge to attack from. The Defender defends from the opposite table edge.

DEPLOYMENT
Both players, starting with the Attacker, take turns placing Units within 12"/30cm of their own table edge until all of their Units are deployed.

WINNING THE GAME
A player wins if their opponent has no Formations left on the table.

FREE FOR ALL

The breakthrough was successful and the situation is fluid. Find and destroy the enemy.

SPECIAL RULES
- Meeting Engagement (Both players)

SETTING UP
The Attacker picks a long table edge to attack from. The Defender defends from the opposite table edge.

Both players, starting with the Attacker, place two Objectives within 8"/20cm of the opponent's table edge, at least 8"/20cm from the side table edges.

DEPLOYMENT
Both players, starting with the Attacker, then take turns placing Units within 12"/30cm of their own table edge until all of their Units are deployed.

WINNING THE GAME
A player wins if they end their turn Holding one of the Objectives that they placed on the opponent's side of the table.

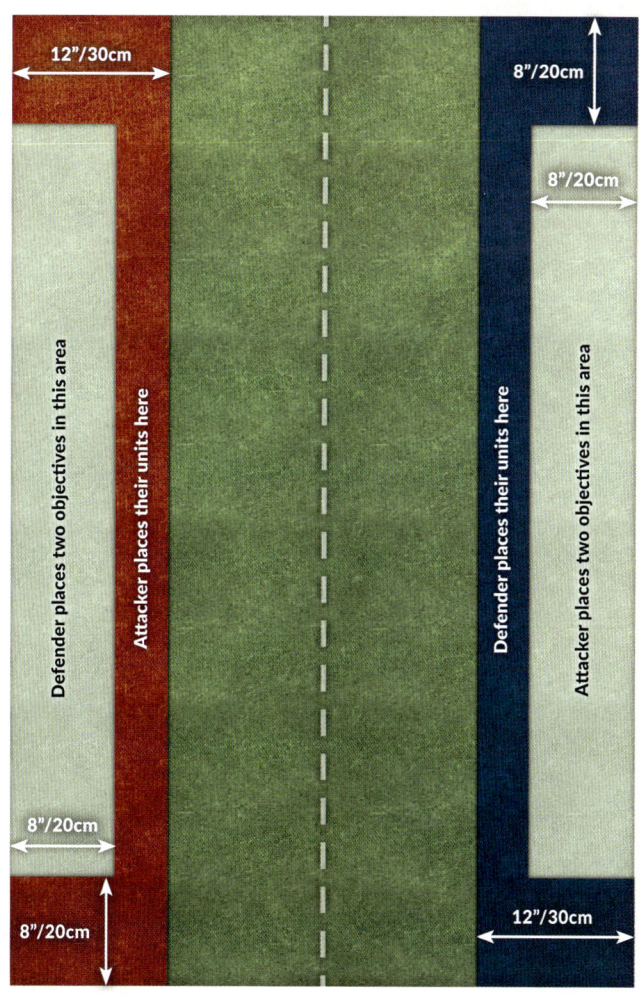

DUST UP

The fighting is confused with the enemy in all directions. Coordinate an attack with your scattered forces.

SPECIAL RULES
- Meeting Engagement (Both players)
- Delayed Reserves (Both players)

SETTING UP
The Attacker picks a table quarter to attack from. The Defender defends from the opposite quarter.

Both players, starting with the Attacker, place one Objective in their own quarter, then both players, again starting with the Attacker, place one Objective in their opponent's quarter. Objectives must be at least 8"/20cm from all table edges and at least 12"/30cm from the table centre.

DEPLOYMENT
Both players place the required part of their force in Delayed Reserve. These Units will arrive from the long table edge adjacent to the player's quarter.

Both players, starting with the Attacker, then take turns placing Units in their own quarters, at least 12"/30cm from the table centre until all of their remaining Units are deployed.

WINNING THE GAME
A player wins if they end their turn Holding one of the Objectives in the opponent's quarter.

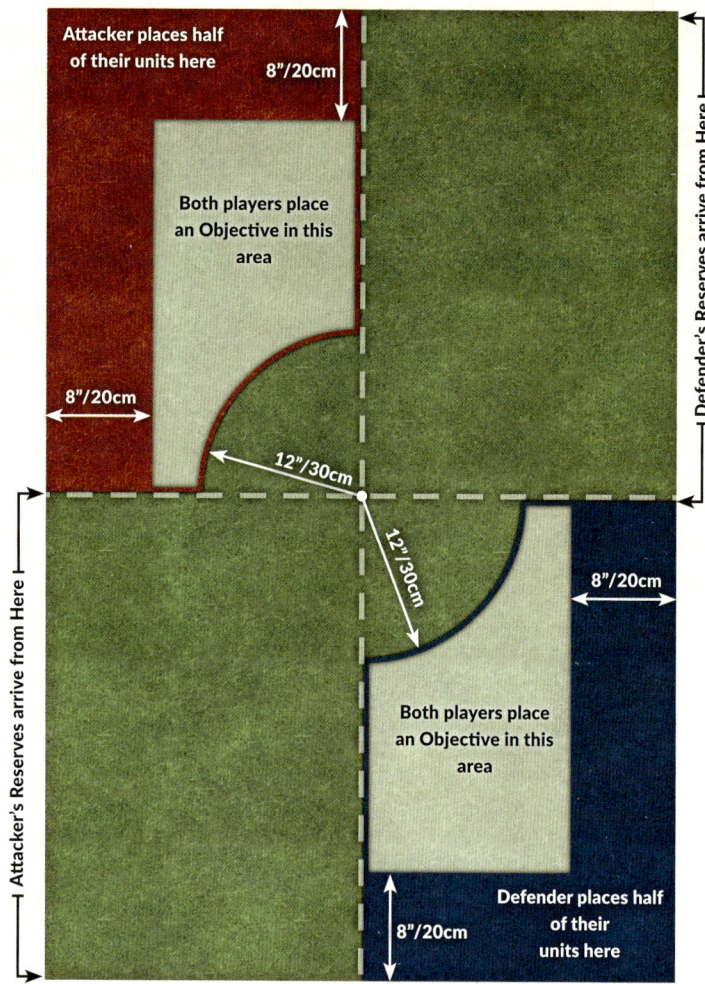

ENCOUNTER

Your forces have been scattered in heavy fighting. Gather your forces and defeat the enemy.

SPECIAL RULES
- Meeting Engagement (Both players)
- Scattered Delayed Reserves (Both players)

SETTING UP
The Attacker picks a long table edge to attack from. The Defender defends from the opposite table edge.

Both players, starting with the Attacker, place two Objectives within 8"/20cm of the opponent's table edge, at least 8"/20cm from the side table edges.

DEPLOYMENT
Both players place the required part of their force in Scattered Delayed Reserve. The players will dice to see where each Unit moves on from as it arrives from reserve.

Both players, starting with the Attacker, then take turns placing Units within 12"/30cm of their own table edge until all of their remaining Units are deployed.

WINNING THE GAME
A player wins if they end their turn Holding one of the Objectives that they placed on the opponent's side of the table.

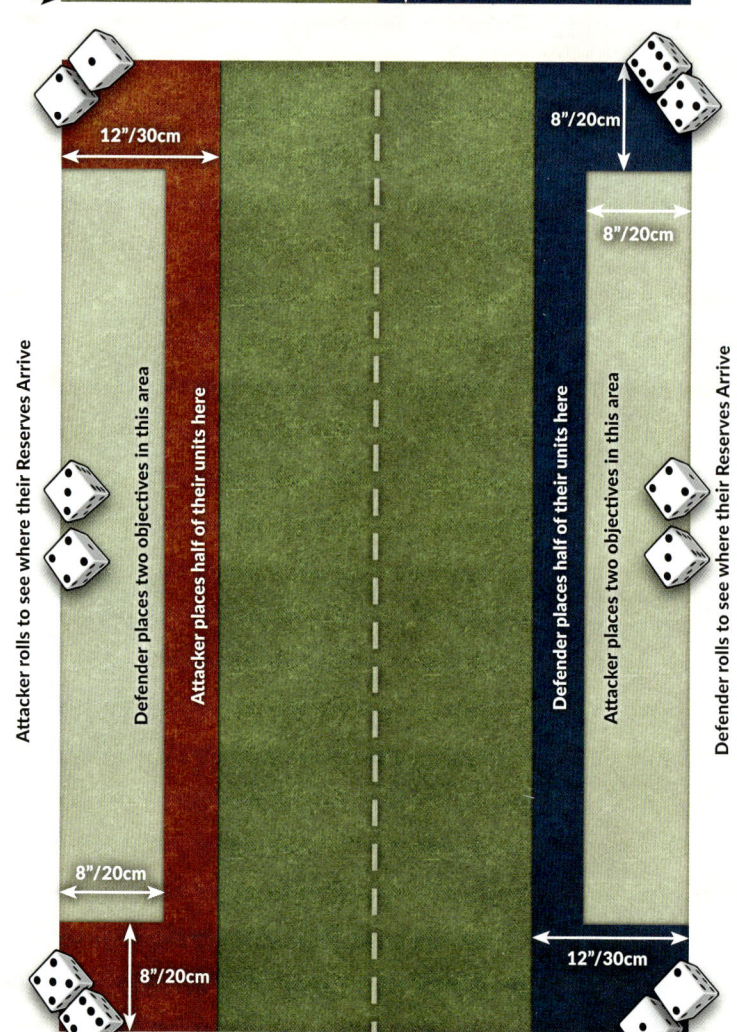

COUNTERATTACK

You have broken through the enemy defences. Beat them to the objective to seal your victory.

SPECIAL RULES
- Ambush (Defender)
- Immediate Reserves (Defender)

SETTING UP

The Defender picks a table quarter to defend. The Attacker picks an adjacent table quarter to attack from.

The Defender places one Objective in their table quarter. The Attacker places one Objective in the quarter diagonally opposite to their own. Objectives must be at least 8"/20cm from all table edges and at least 12"/30cm from the centre.

DEPLOYMENT

The Defender places the required part of their force in Immediate Reserve and may hold one of their remaining Units in Ambush. They then place their remaining Units in their quarter at least 12"/30cm from the table centre. Reserves arrive within 16"/40cm of the opposite corner.

The Attacker places all of their Units in their table quarter at least 8"/20cm from both centrelines.

WINNING THE GAME

The game cannot be won before the sixth turn. The Attacker wins if they end their turn Holding an Objective. The Defender wins if they end their turn with no Attacking Tank or Infantry Teams within 8"/20cm of an Objective.

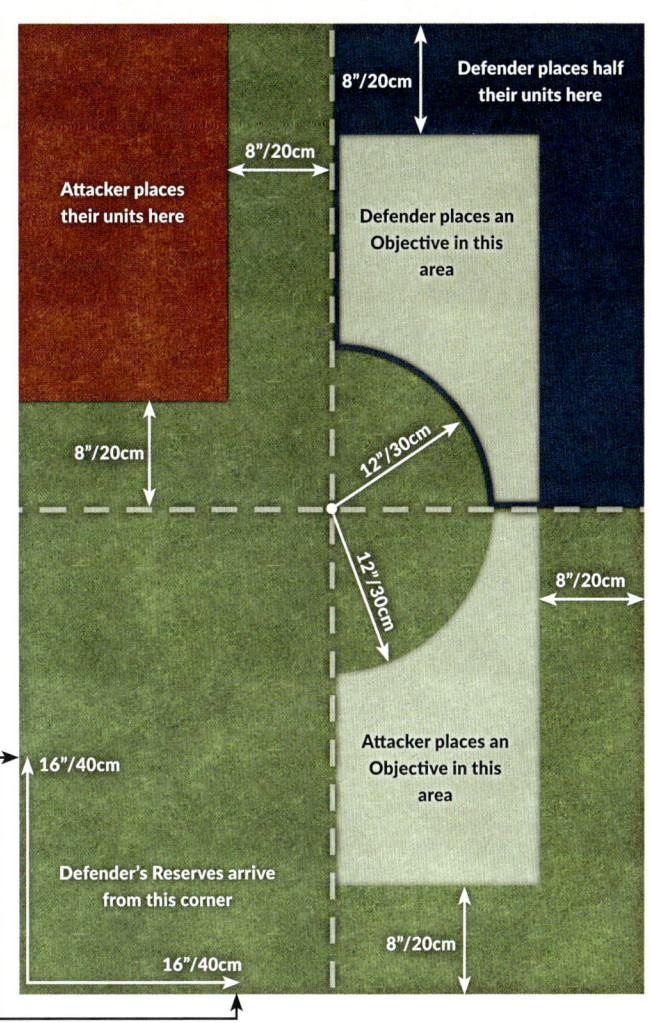

CONTACT

Your advance has contacted the enemy before their defences are prepared. Attack before they can reinforce.

SPECIAL RULES
- Ambush (Defender)
- Immediate Reserves (Attacker)
- Scattered Delayed Reserves (Defender)

SETTING UP

The Defender picks a long table edge to defend. The Attacker attacks from the opposite table edge.

The Defender two Objectives in the Attacker's table half at least 16"/40cm from the centre line. The Attacker now places two Objectives in the Defender's table half, at least 12"/30cm from the centre line. All Objectives must be at least 8"/20cm from the side table edges.

DEPLOYMENT

The Defender places the required part of their force in Scattered Delayed Reserve and may hold one Unit in Ambush. They then place their remaining Units in their table half at least 8"/20cm from the centre line.

The Attacker places the required part of their force in Immediate Reserve, then places their remaining Units in their table half at least 12"/30cm from the centre line.

WINNING THE GAME

A player wins if they end their turn Holding one of the Objectives on the opponent's side of the table.

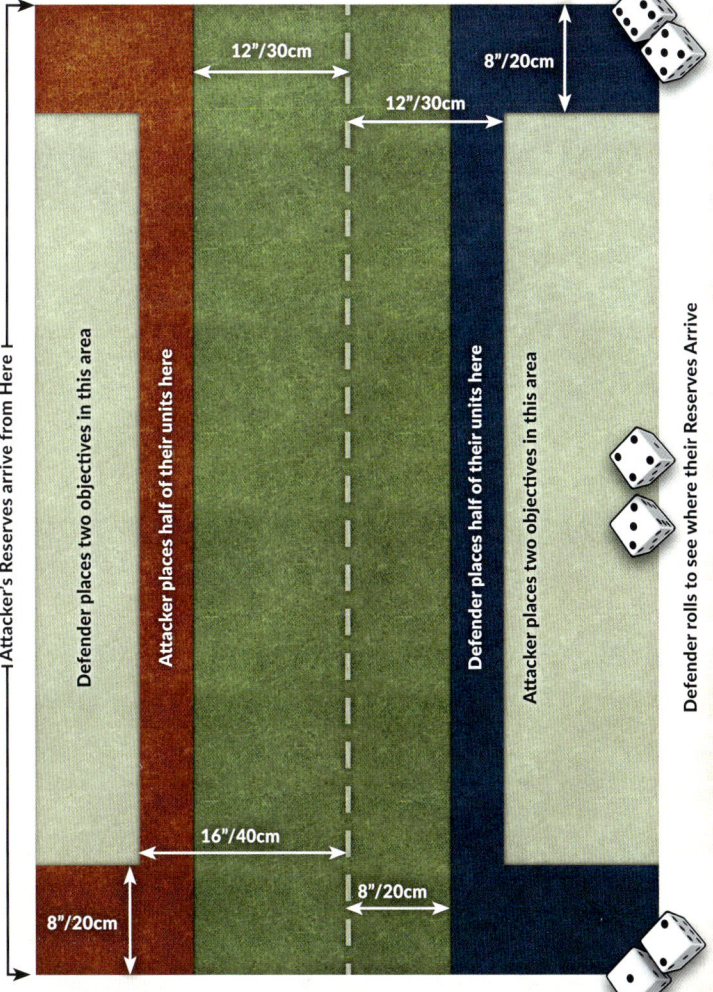

MORE MISSIONS

These missions are a little more complex than the basic missions in the previous section, adding new twists and challenges for you to overcome. With the addition of minefields, different reserves rules, and strategic withdrawal—where the defender slowly removes parts of their force as they thin out the rearguard, there is lots to try out.

BREAKTHROUGH

You have outflanked the enemy. Seize the objectives before they can redeploy to protect them.

SPECIAL RULES
- Ambush (Defender)
- Immediate Reserves (Defender)
- Flanking Delayed Reserves (Attacker)

SETTING UP
The Defender picks two diagonally opposite table quarters to defend. The Attacker picks a quarter to attack from.

The Attacker places two Objectives in the remaining table quarter at least 8"/20cm from all table edges.

DEPLOYMENT
The Defender places the required part of their force in Immediate Reserve and may hold one Unit in Ambush. Reserves arrive within 16"/40cm of either of their table corners. They then place their remaining Units in their table quarters, divided as they wish.

The Attacker places at least one Unit in Delayed Reserve. These will arrive within 16"/40cm of the Objective table corner. They then place the remaining Units in their table quarter at least 8"/20cm from both centrelines.

WINNING THE GAME
The game cannot be won before the sixth turn. The Attacker wins if they end their turn Holding an Objective. The Defender wins if they end their turn with no Attacking Tank or Infantry teams within 8"/20cm of an Objective.

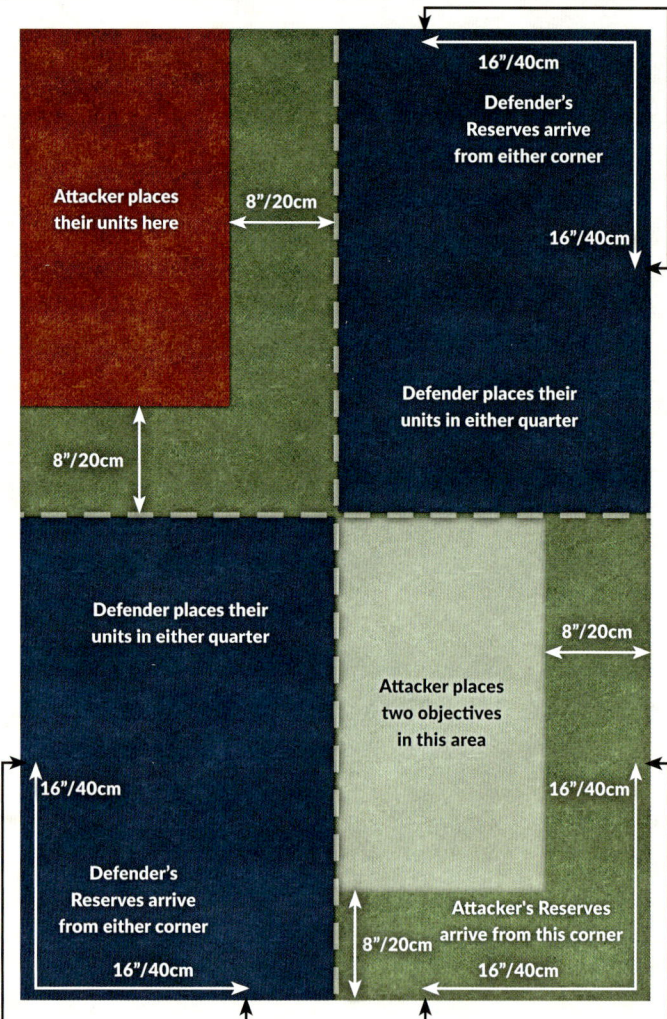

REARGUARD

You have the enemy on the run. Don't let them get away.

SPECIAL RULES
- Ambush (Defender)
- Strategic Withdrawal (Defender)

SETTING UP
The Defender picks a long table edge to defend. The Attacker attacks from the opposite table edge.

The Attacker places two Objectives within 16"/40cm of the Defender's edge and at least 16"/40cm from the sides.

The Defender places one Minefield outside the opponent's deployment area for each 25 points in their force.

DEPLOYMENT
The Defender may hold a Unit in Ambush and places their remaining Units in their table half.

The Attacker places all of their Units within 8"/20cm of their table edge.

STRATEGIC WITHDRAWAL
The Defender will remove Units from their force as the game progresses using the Strategic Withdrawal rule (page 86).

WINNING THE GAME
The Attacker wins if they end their turn Holding one of the Objectives. The Defender wins at the start of their ninth turn after checking Formation Morale.

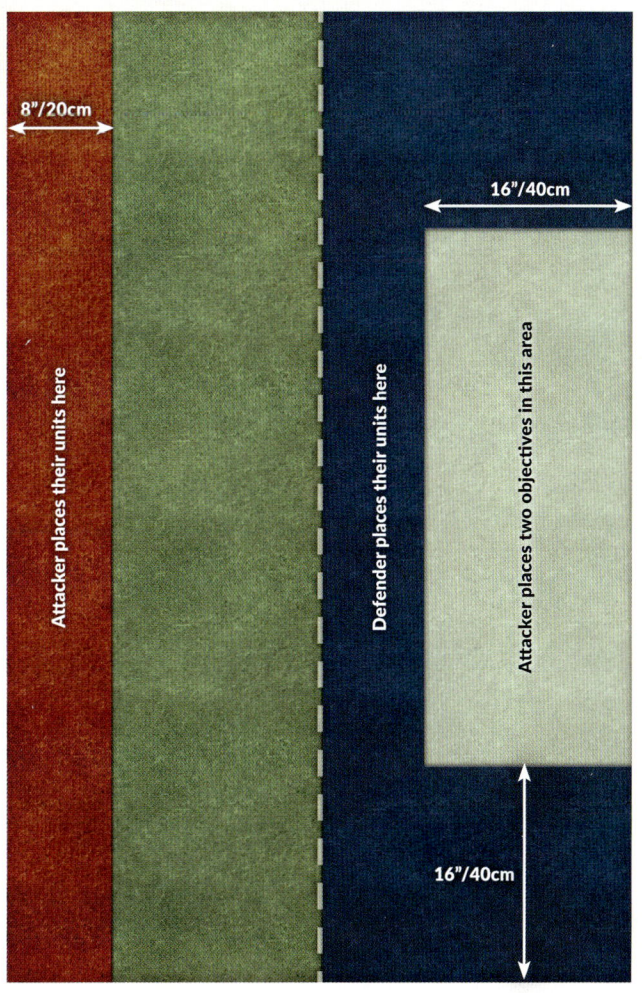

NO RETREAT

The enemy are on the defensive, smash them before their reserves can arrive and save them.

SPECIAL RULES
- Ambush (Defender)
- Deep Immediate Reserves (Defender)

SETTING UP
The Defender picks a short table edge to defend from. The Attacker attacks from the opposite edge.

Both players, starting with the Defender, place one Objective in the Defender's table half, at least 8"/20cm from the table centre line and all table edges.

The Defender places one Minefield outside the opponent's deployment area for each 25 points in their force.

DEPLOYMENT
The Defender places the required part of their force in Deep Immediate Reserve and may hold one Unit in Ambush. Reserves arrive from their short table edge.

The Defender places their Units in their table half.

The Attacker places all of their Units in their table half at least 16"/40cm from the table centre line.

WINNING THE GAME
The Attacker wins if they end their turn Holding an Objective. The Defender wins if they end their turn on or after the sixth turn with no Attacking Tank or Infantry teams within 8"/20cm of an Objective.

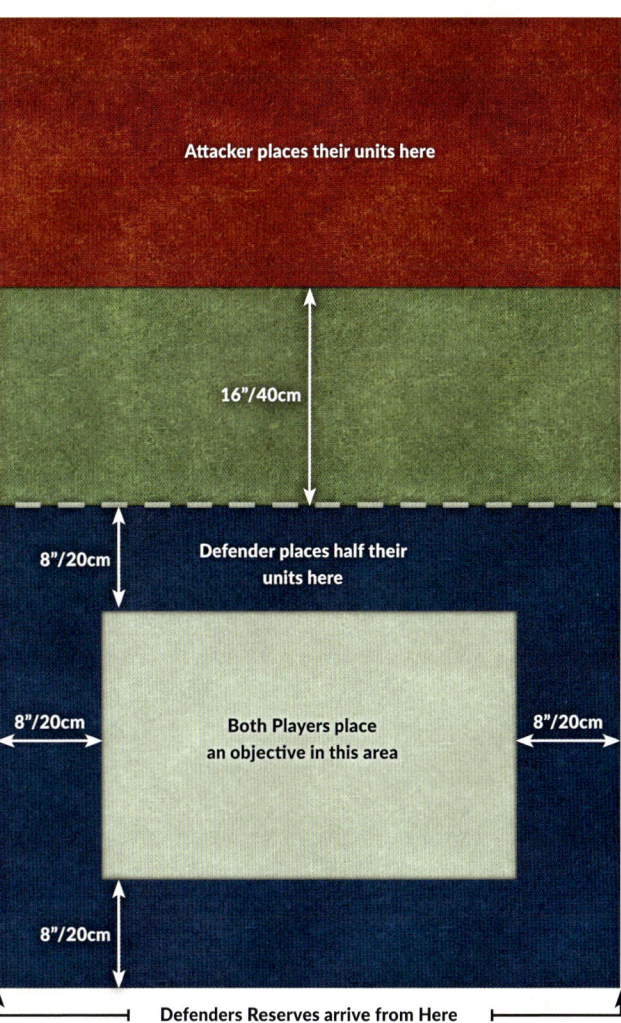

BRIDGEHEAD

The enemy has forced a bridgehead across a river with light troops. Cut them off and destroy them.

SPECIAL RULES
- Ambush (Defender)
- Deep Scattered Immediate Reserves (Defender)

SETTING UP
The Defender picks a long table edge to defend from. The Attacker attacks from the opposite edge.

The Attacker places two Objectives at least 8"/20cm from the centre line, at least 8"/20cm from the long table edge, and at least 28"/70cm from the short table edges.

The Defender places one Minefield outside the opponent's deployment area for each 25 points in their force.

DEPLOYMENT
The Defender places the required part of their force in Deep Scattered Immediate Reserve and may hold one Unit in Ambush. They place their remaining Units in their half at least 20"/50cm from the side edges.

The Attacker places their Units at least 16"/40cm from the centre line or within 8"/20cm of the side edge.

WINNING THE GAME
The Attacker wins if they end their turn Holding an Objective. The Defender wins if they end their turn on or after the sixth turn with no Attacking Tank or Infantry teams within 8"/20cm of an Objective.

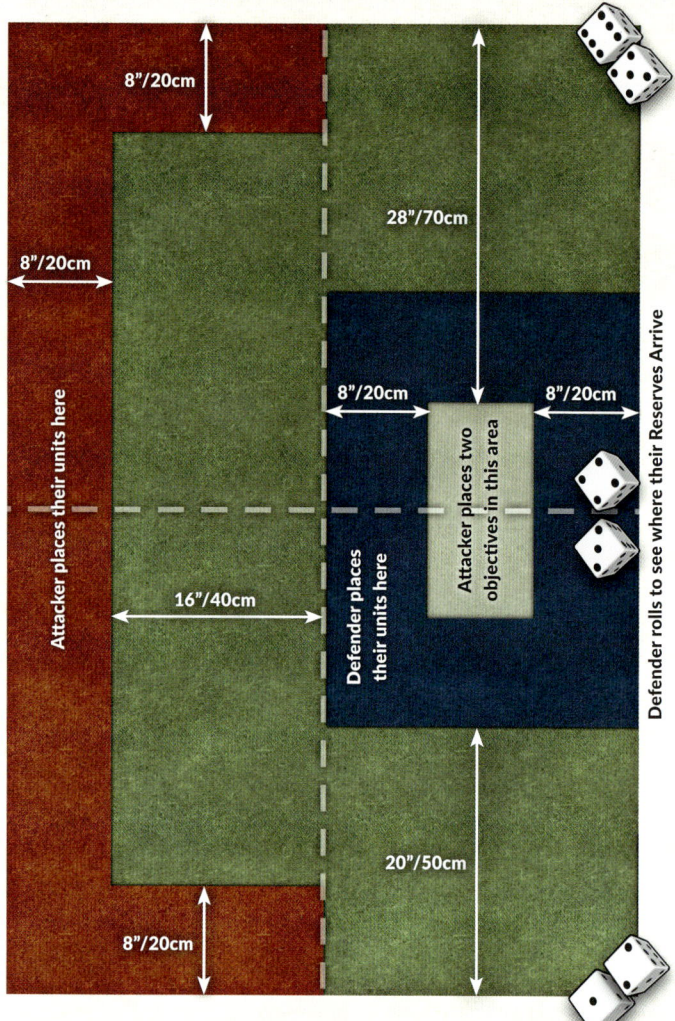

NIGHT FIGHTING

The Russian soldiers dropped down and began to exchange fire with the infantry. The disabled tank attempted to support from where it was by firing its main gun, but it did little good. There began a deadly game of hide and seek. The Russians, lacking night vision devices, waited until an American infantryman fired. When he fired his first few shots, the Russian would orient his weapon to the general location that he had seen the muzzle flash. If the American did not move before he fired again, the Russian would take aim and fire a burst. Doing this, however, exposed the Russians to the same risks and results. So the infantry battle bogged down into a fire fight with sporadic and violent exchanges of gunfire followed by brief pauses as both sides tried to fix new targets, followed again by a new exchange of gunfire as someone found a mark and fired.

MOVING AT NIGHT
Teams may not move faster than their Terrain Dash speed at Night. In addition, Teams add +1 to their Cross number when moving through Difficult Terrain at night.

SHOOTING AT NIGHT
Teams Shooting at Night always suffer an additional +1 penalty on the score needed To Hit, unless the shooting Team has Thermal Imaging.

LINE OF SIGHT AT NIGHT
Units must roll on the Night Visibility Table to determine their maximum Line of Sight distance. Teams from a Unit do not have Line of Sight to Teams beyond the rolled distance. Roll immediately before checking Line of Sight.

TARGET SHOT LAST TURN
The maximum distance does not limit Line of Sight to enemy Teams that Shot in their previous Shooting step.

Shooting at Night token

SHOOTING AT NIGHT

The T-72 and infantry teams want to shoot the M113. As it is night, they must roll to see how far they can see. The T-72 has Infra-red equipment, so rolls two dice and takes the best.

The infantry roll high enough to see the M113, so can shoot it. The T-72 did not. However, since the M1 Abrams fired last turn, the T-72 can see it at any distance.

NIGHT VISION DEVICES

Night vision devices like Infra-Red and Thermal Imaging give troops a significant advantage in battles fought at night, making targets easier to find (see page 68).

BOMBARDMENTS AT NIGHT

Spotting Teams do not need to roll on the Night Visibility Table. Their Line of Sight is not affected by Night. However, attempts to Range In at Night add +1 to the score needed.

NIGHT VISIBILITY TABLE	
DIE ROLL	DISTANCE
1	4"/10cm
2	8"/20cm
3	12"/30cm
4	16"/40cm
5	20"/50cm
6	24"/60cm

TIME OF DAY

You can play games in four light conditions or times of day. You can chose to play any of your games at one of these times: Dawn, Daylight, Dusk, and Darkness.

DAWN

In a game that starts at night using the Dawn rules, the Defender rolls a die at the start of their third turn:

- On a score of 5+, morning has broken. Once morning breaks, the Night Fighting rules are no longer used, and the rest of the battle is fought in Daylight.
- If the roll is unsuccessful, at the start of the Attacker's turn four, they roll two dice with morning breaking on any roll of 5+.
- If it is still dark at the start of the Defender's next turn, they roll three dice, and so on with each player rolling one more die until morning breaks on any roll of 5+.

DAYLIGHT

In a game being played in Daylight, the Night Fighting rules are not used.

DUSK

In a game being played at Dusk, the game starts in Daylight.

At the start of the Defender's third turn, roll a die:

- On a score of 5+, night has fallen. Once night falls, the Night Fighting rules come into effect and the rest of the battle is fought in Darkness.
- If the roll is unsuccessful, at the start of the Attacker's turn four, they roll two dice with night falling on any roll of 5+.
- If it is still light at the start of the Defender's next turn, they roll three dice, and so on with each player rolling one more die until night falls on any roll of 5+.

DARKNESS

In a game being played in Darkness, the entire game is played using the Night Fighting rules.

USING TIME OF DAY AND NIGHT FIGHTING IN MISSIONS

The Attacker in any Mission may choose to either roll on the Random Time of Day Table, or to Attack in Daylight.

RANDOM TIME OF DAY	
DIE ROLL	MISSION
1 or 2	Dawn
3 or 4	Daylight
5 or 6	Dusk

MINEFIELDS

Tanks began to hit the mines, shedding tracks severed by the detonation and stopping. Belatedly, it occurred to them they were in a minefield, an unexpected inconvenience but one that they could deal with. The companies began to reform into columns behind tanks equipped with mine plows and rollers. Once out of the minefield, they would redeploy and continue as before. It was a battle drill they had rehearsed many times before and were able to carry out with little trouble. It was at this point, when the Soviets were in the midst of redeploying, that Major Jordan ordered Delta Company, the ITVs, and Team Bravo to open fire. The sudden mass volley caught the Soviets off-guard.

The location of a Minefield is shown by a Minefield marker. Any Team moving within 2"/5cm of a Minefield marker risks being knocked out.

A Team that then Moves into a Minefield must roll a die.
- If the score is at least equal to the Unit's Skill rating, the Team crosses the Minefield safely.
- Otherwise, the Team was hit by a mine with Anti-tank 5 and Firepower 1+ and must take a Save to survive (using its Top armour if it is a Tank Team) (pages 46 to 48). If a Tank Team is Bailed Out or Destroyed, it halts in the middle of the Minefield. If it survives, it continues moving unharmed.

A Unit that took hits from a Minefield will be Pinned Down (page 50) when it finishes moving.

CLEARING A MINEFIELD

A Unit Leader that is not Pinned Down may issue a Mine Clearing Order as a Movement Order instead of Moving in the Movement Step.

If it does so, any Tank Team with a Mine Clearing Device (such as a plough, rollers, or flail) or any Infantry Team from the Unit within 6"/15cm of the Unit Leader may immediately remove a Minefield within 2"/5cm (having moved into the Minefield on a previous turn) instead of Moving. The Team is counted as Moving, but does not Move, and cannot Move further, Shoot or Assault.

Minefield token

CROSSING MINEFIELDS

A T-72 Tank Company attempts to cross some Minefields. They must pass a Skill test to avoid the mines. One passes through safely on a roll of 5.
The two that failed on rolls of 2 and 3 then roll Armour Saves, one passes while the other fails and is destroyed.

BATTLE PLANS

The Battle Plans mission selector has players pick a plan that will influence the type of mission they will play. Before the game, the NATO and Warsaw Pact players each secretly pick a battle plan (Attack, Manoeuvre, or Defend).

They then reveal and compare their plans on the Battle Plans table below and roll a die to see what mission to play.

BATTLE PLANS

NATO PLAYER'S PLAN	WARSAW PACT PLAYER'S PLAN		
	ATTACK	MANOEUVRE	DEFEND
ATTACK	Roll to see who Attacks 1: Breakthrough 2: Counterattack 3: Dust Up 4: Encounter 5: Free for All 6: Free for All	NATO Player Attacks Warsaw Pact Player Defends 1: Breakthrough 2: Contact 3: Counterattack 4: Counterattack 5: Dust Up 6: Encounter	NATO Player Attacks Warsaw Pact Player Defends 1 or 2: Bridgehead 3 or 4: No Retreat 5 or 6: Rearguard
MANOEUVRE	Warsaw Pact Player Attacks NATO Player Defends 1: Breakthrough 2: Contact 3: Counterattack 4: Counterattack 5: Dust Up 6: Encounter	Roll to see who Attacks 1: Breakthrough 2: Counterattack 3: Dust Up 4: Encounter 5: Free for All 6: Free for All	NATO Player Attacks Warsaw Pact Player Defends 1: Breakthrough 2: Bridgehead 3: Contact 4: No Retreat 5: No Retreat 6: Rearguard
DEFEND	Warsaw Pact Player Attacks NATO Player Defends 1 or 2: Bridgehead 3 or 4: No Retreat 5 or 6: Rearguard	Warsaw Pact Player Attacks NATO Player Defends 1: Breakthrough 2: Bridgehead 3: Contact 4: No Retreat 5: No Retreat 6: Rearguard	Roll to see who Attacks 1: Breakthrough 2: Counterattack 3: Dust Up 4: Encounter 5: Free for All 6: Free for All

WHY SELECT ATTACK

When you choose the Attack Battle Plan, you can be fairly sure that you will be attacking in a fairly straightforward mission. This suits forces that rely on brute force over mobility. You will be able to focus your firepower to reduce the enemy piece by piece as you advance into their defensive position.

WHY SELECT MANOEUVRE

A Manoeuvre Battle plan allows you to exploit your mobility while avoiding assaults against fortified positions. This suits forces that have a good mix of mobility and firepower. You won't be trapped into a grinding battle of attrition, and can manoeuvre rapidly to defeat your opponent.

WHY SELECT DEFEND

A Defend battle plan allows you to dig in and force the enemy to come to you. You can lay out a carefully planned defence with interlocking fields of fire covering selected killing zones without needing to worry about manoeuvring light troops across open ground. This suits infantry forces with a good anti-tank missile capability.

INDEX

ALPHA
AA (Anti-aircraft) 29, 39, 44, 48, 66
AA MG 66
Accurate 66
Advanced Stabilisers 66
Aircraft . 18, 23, 29, 39, 44, 48
   Arrival 29
   Bombardments 51-54
   Concealment 42
   Deep Reserves 78
   Line of Sight 41
   Helicopters 18, 39, 42, 44, 69
   Hunter-killer . . 18, 42, 44, 69
   Landed 35, 39
   Loitering Off Table . . 29, 78
   Meeting Engagements . . 78
   Roll for Strike Aircraft . . 29
   Safety Distance 43
   Shooting At 39, 44, 48
   Strike Aircraft . . . .
                      18, 23, 29, 69
   Transport Aircraft 35
Aircraft Saves 23, 48
Allied Support 65, 77, 78
Ambush 29, 85
Amphibious 68
Annihilation mission 87
Anti-Helicopter 39, 44, 66
Anti-tank Rating . . . 38, 46, 47
Armoured Tanks 18, 21, 46-47, 50, 54
Armour Saves 46-47, 54, 60, 61
Artillery 21, 51-56
   Aiming Point 52
   Bulletproof Cover 54
   Danger Close 53
   Meeting Engagements . . 78
   Pre-planned 54
   Range In 53
   Repeat Bombardments . . 54
   Roll to Hit 53
   Rotate to Face 53
   Smoke Bombardments . . 56
   Spotting Team 51-53
   Templates 52-53
Assault # 69
Assaults 29, 57-63
   Break Off 62, 63
   Charge into Contact . . . . . .
                      57, 58, 62
   Consolidating 63
   Counterattack 61, 62
   Defensive Fire 59, 60
   Falling Back 60
   Is Assault Over 61
   Roll Saves 61
   Roll to Hit 60
   Shooting Before 57
   Sneaking Up on Tanks . . 59
   Through Terrain 58
   Transport Teams 61
   Unarmoured Tank
      Teams 57
Attachments 19, 22, 64, 83, 78

BRAVO
Bailed Out . . 29, 47, 60, 61, 64
Battle Plans 95
Bazooka Skirts 68
BDD Armour 68
Blitz Move 36
Bombardments . see Artillery
Bomblets 55
Break Off 62, 63
Breakthrough mission 91
Bridgehead mission 92
Brutal 66
Buildings 25, 26, 33, 41, 42, 48
   Concealment 41, 42
   Line of Sight 40, 42
Bulletproof Cover . . 48, 54, 60

CHARLIE
Charge into Contact 57, 58, 62
Chobham Armour 68
Commander 19, 47, 50, 57, 62, 65
   Changing Tanks 49
   Formation Morale 65
   Assaulting 57
   Command Leadership . . 47, 50, 62, 64
   Joining Units 57
   Killing Commanders . . . 49
   Unit Morale 64
Command Leadership 47, 50, 62, 64
Concealment 41, 42
   Score to Hit 44
Consolidating 63
Contact mission 89
Counterattack mission 89
Counterattack in assault . . 62
Cross Check 21, 32, 33
Cross Here 37

DELTA
Danger Close 53
Dash Speed 30, 44, 92
Dawn 93
Dedicated AA 66
Deep Reserves 78
Defensive Fire 59
Delayed Reserves 78
Deployment 83
   Spearhead 69
Difficult Terrain . . . 24, 32, 37
Digging In 37, 48, 54, 63,
   At Deployment 83
Dismounting Transports . . 34
Dragon Mount 68
Draws, Victory Points 83
Dust Up mission 88

ECHO
Encounter mission 88
ERA Armour 68

FOXTROT
Falling Back 60
Firepower 38, 47, 48, 54
Field of Fire 43, 53, 66
Follow Me 36
Force Diagrams 77, 78
Formation Morale . . 29, 65, 83
Formations 19, 76, 78
   Allied 65, 77, 78
   Cards 20, 78
   Commander 19
   Formation Diagrams 76
   HQ Unit 19
   Multiple Formations 19, 65, 77
   Support 77, 78
Forward Firing 66
Foxholes 37, 48, 54, 63
   At Deployment 83
Free for All mission 87

GOLF
Gaps 32, 40
Gone to Ground . . 30, 44, 54
   At Deployment 83
Good Spirits, In 64, 65
Guided 66
Guided AA 66
Guided Missiles 66
   Helicopters, shooting at . 39

HOTEL
Halted ROF 39, 44, 57, 59
Hammerhead 68
HEAT 66
Heavy Weapon . 18, 39, 57, 68
Helicopters 18, 29, 35, 39, 42-44, 69
Hills 25, 26, 33
   Concealment 41, 42
Line of Sight 40, 41
HQ Transport 69
HQ Units 19, 45, 64, 76
Hunter-killer 18, 42, 69

INDIA
Immediate Reserves 78
In Command 31
In Good Spirits 64, 65, 83
Independent 19, 45, 69
Infantry Saves 22, 48
   None in Assaults 61
   Brutal Weapons 66
   Repeat Bombardments . . 54
Infantry Teams . 18, 38, 48, 54
   Aircraft, shooting at . 39, 48
   Concealed In Flat Terrain 42
   In Good Spirits 64
   Guided cannot hit 66
   Pinned Down 50
   Saves 48, 54, 61
   Sneaking Up on Tanks . . 59
   Start in Foxholes 83
Infantry Units 22
Infra-red (IR) 68

JULIET
Joining Units 57

LIMA
Landed Aircraft . . . .
                 35, 39, 42, 49
Laser Rangefinder 66
Laser-Guided Projectiles . . 55
Leaving the Table 29, 83
Left Out of Battle 83
Line of Sight 40-42, 50, 54, 56, 66
Loitering Off Table 29, 78

MIKE
Machine-guns (MG) 38
Meeting Engagements 78
Mine Clearing Devices . . . 68
Minefields 94
   Clearing 94
Minelets 55
Missions 87-91
   Annihilation 87
   Bridgehead 92
   Breakthrough 91
   Contact 89
   Counterattack 89
   Dust up 88
   Encounter 88
   Free For All 87
   No Retreat 91

Rearguard 90
Mistaken Target. 45
Morale 29, 64, 65, 83
Mounting Transports. 34
Movement 29, 30
   Aircraft 29
   Cross Check 32
   Cross Here 37
   Cross Number 21
   Dash Speed. 30, 32
   Difficult Terrain. 32
   In Command 31
   Minefields. 94
   Near the Enemy. 31
   Night 92
   Orders 36
   Out of Command 31
   Speed Chart 20
   Tactical Speed. 30
   Through Gaps 32
   Through Teams 31
   Through Terrain 32
Moving Through Teams 31, 57
Moving ROF 39, 44, 78

NOVEMBER

Night Fighting. 68, 92
   Ranging In 54
   Score to Hit. 44
Night Visibility Table 92
No Retreat mission. 91

OSCAR

Objectives. 54, 83, 84
Observer. 51, 53, 55, 69
One Shot. 66
Out of Command 31, 44
Overhead Fire 67

PAPA

Passenger #. 68
Passengers 34
   Assaults 61
   Capacity. 34, 68
   Deployment 83
   On Tanks. 34, 35
   Reserves. 78
   Shooting at 35
Pinned Down 29, 50, 54
   Assaults 60, 63
Pinned ROF 1 67
Points 20, 78
Pre-planned Artillery. 54

ROMEO

Radar 67
Rally from
   Pinned Down . . 29, 50
Random Missions. 82
Range 38, 40, 51
   Minimum Range 40

Radar 67
Range In 53, 54, 56
Rate of Fire (ROF) 38
Rearguard mission 91
Recoilless 67
Remount Bailed Out . . 29, 47
Repeating Bombardments. 54
Replacing Unit Leaders . . . 49
Reserves. 29, 78
   Deep 78
   Delayed 78
   Flanking 78
   Immediate. 78
   Scattered 78
ROF (Rate of Fire) 38, 44
   Anti-aircraft 44
   Slow Firing 67
Roll for Strike Aircraft 29
Roll to Hit. 44, 53, 60
Rotate to Face 43, 53

SIERRA

Safety Distance 43
Salvo 51
Saves 46-48, 54, 61
   Aircraft 48
   Armour Saves 46-47, 54, 61
   Assaults 61
   Infantry 48
   Tank 46-47
   Repeat Bombardments. . 54
   Unarmoured Tank. 48
Scattered Reserves 78
Score to Hit 44, 54
Scout 44, 69
Shoot and Scoot 37
Shooting. 29, 38
   Armour Saves. 46-47
   Bailed Out. 29, 47
   Before Assaulting. 57
   Bulletproof Cover 48
   Check Line of Sight. 40
   Check Range. 40
   Commanders 49
   Concealment 41, 42
   Dash Speed,
      no shooting. 44
   Declare Targets. 43
   Defensive Fire. 59
   Mistaken Target 45
   Night 44, 53, 68, 92
   Out of Command 44
   Passengers. 35
   Pinned Down. 29, 50
   Range. 38, 40, 44
   Roll Saves 46-48
   Roll to Hit. 44
   Rotate to Face. 43
   Score to Hit. 44
   Smoke 44, 50, 53, 56

Short Terrain 26, 33, 41
Side Armour 46, 60, 61
Slow Firing. 67
Smoke 29, 50, 67
   Range In 53
   Score to Hit. 44
Smoke Bombardment . 56, 67
Sneaking Up on Tanks. . . . 59
Spearhead. 69
Spotting Team 51-54
Stabiliser. 67
Strategic Withdrawal 78
Strike Aircraft . .18, 23, 29, 69
Support Units 65, 77, 78

TANGO

Tactical Speed 30
   Advanced Stabilisers. . . . 66
   Stabiliser 67
   Through Terrain 32
Tall Terrain. 26, 33, 41, 42
Tank Saves 46-47, 54, 61
Tank Teams 18, 20,
         38, 46-47, 54
   Armoured. . . 18, 21, 46-47,
        50, 54, 60, 61
   Cannot Assault Tanks. . . 57
   Falling Back 60
   In Good Spirits. 64
   Saves 46-47, 54, 61
   Sneaking Up on 59
   Unarmoured. . . . 18, 48, 50,
      54, 57, 61, 68
Tank Units 20
   Deep Reserves 78
Templates 52
Terrain 24-27, 33
   Assaulting across 58
   Concealed by .41, 42, 69, 85
   Cross Check 32, 37
   Cross Here 37
   Difficult Terrain . . 24, 32, 37
   Impassable 25, 32
   Movement through 32
   Ranging In Near 53
   Terrain Chart 33
Thermal Imaging . . 50, 56, 68
Too Close for Error. 45
Top Armour. 54, 61, 94
Transport Teams 18,
          34-35, 64
   Aircraft 35
   Assaults 61
   Dismounting 34
   Mounting 34

Transport Units. 22, 23
   Attachments 19, 22, 23,
       64, 83, 85, 78
   Ambushes 85

Bring Forward 35
Deployment 83
Reserves. 78
Send to Rear 35
Turreted Tank 46

UNIFORM

Unarmoured Saves . . . .
        48, 61, 68
Unarmoured Tanks 18,
        48, 54, 68
   No Charge
      into Contact . . . 57, 68
   Pinned Down. 50, 54
   No Saves in Assaults 61
Unit Cards 20-23
Unit Leader 19
   Replacing 49
Unit Morale 64
   Commander's Leadership 64
Units 19, 20
   Cards 20-23
   HQ Units. 19, 45, 64, 76
   Independent Units. . . . .
        19, 45, 69
   Support Units . . . .
        65, 77, 78
Unit Structure 20

VICTOR

Victory Conditions. . . . 83, 84
Victory Points 83

WHISKEY

Weapons. 39, 66-67
   Accurate 66
   Advanced Stabilisers. . . . 66
   Anti-aircraft (AA). 39,
        44, 48, 66
   Anti-Helicopter . . 39, 44, 66
   Artillery. 51
   Dedicated AA. . . . 39, 44, 66
   Guided. 39, 66
   Guided AA 66
   Hammerhead 68
   HEAT. 66
   Laser Rangefinder 66
   One Shot 66
   Slow Firing 67
   Smoke 50
   Smoke Bombardment. . . 56
   Stabiliser 67
   Which Can Fire 38
Weapons Characteristics . . . .
       20, 22, 38
Wrecks 33, 49, 64
WYSIWYG. 17, 27

STARTING

STARTING STEP (P. 29)
1. Remount Bailed Out Tanks
2. Rally Pinned Down Units
3. Check Unit Morale
4. Check Formation Morale
5. Reveal Ambushes
6. Roll for Reserves
7. Roll for Strike Aircraft
8. Remove Friendly Smoke Markers

REMOUNT BAILED OUT TANKS (P. 47)
May not Move, Shoot, Bombard, or Assault. If Bailed Out again, pass Motivation (or Remount) or Destroyed. Score Remount to Remount.

RALLY PINNED DOWN UNITS (P. 50)
Shoot with Moving ROF, cannot Move closer to visible enemy or Bombard. Score Rally to Rally.

CHECK UNIT MORALE (P. 64)
In Good Spirits if:
- No Teams Bailed Out or Destroyed, or
- 2 or more Tanks (not Bailed Out), or
- 3 or more Infantry Teams remain.

If not In Good Spirits, score Morale or Unit is Destroyed.

CHECK FORMATION MORALE (P. 65)
If Formation doesn't have at least two Units on table or in Reserve, it is Destroyed.

REVEAL AMBUSHES (P. 85)
Place Teams in Deployment Area, not within 4"/10cm of enemy, 16"/40cm if in Line of Sight unless Concealed by Terrain.

ROLL FOR RESERVES (P. 86)
Roll one die first turn of Reserves, two dice second turn, three dice third turn, etc. Each score of 5+ brings on a Unit.

ROLL FOR STRIKE AIRCRAFT (P. 29)
On a score of 4+, a Unit of Aircraft arrives until the end of the turn.

MOVEMENT

STAYING IN COMMAND (P. 31)
In Command if end movement:
- within 6"/15cm of Unit Leader, or
- within 8"/20cm of Unit Leader if Unit has eight or more Teams.

OUT OF COMMAND (P. 31)
If not In Command, Team must:
- remain in place,
- Move at Tactical with +1 penalty on score To Hit when Shooting, or
- Move at Dash towards Unit Leader.

MOVING THROUGH TERRAIN (P. 32)
Move at Tactical and Shoot or Assault, or Move at Terrain Dash.

DIFFICULT TERRAIN (P. 32)
Score Cross rating or stop Moving (Team has still Moved).

CROSSING MINEFIELDS (P. 94)
If Moving within 2"/5cm of Minefield marker, score Skill to avoid mines, otherwise hit. Mines are Anti-tank 5 and Firepower 1+ (hit Top armour if Armoured Tank).

MOVEMENT ORDERS (P. 36)
Unit Leader can issue one Order per turn to Teams that are In Command.

BLITZ MOVE — BEFORE MOVING
Score Skill to Move Teams up to 4"/10cm. Can only Move at Tactical this turn. If do not Move further, Shoot with Halted ROF.
Otherwise, Teams from the Unit cannot Dash and suffer the +1 to hit penalty for Moving Out of Command.

CROSS HERE — WHILE MOVING
Teams Crossing Difficult Terrain reduce Cross rating by 1 within 6"/15cm of Leader.

FOLLOW ME! — AFTER MOVING
Move Unit Leader forward 4"/10cm, then Score Courage to Move Teams forward 4"/10cm.
Pass or fail, teams that are In Command cannot Shoot.

SHOOT AND SCOOT — ASSAULT STEP
Score Skill to Move Teams that did not Move, up to 4"/10cm.

DIG IN — MOVEMENT STEP
Score Skill to dig Foxholes. Teams then Shoot with Moving ROF, but cannot fire Bombardments.

MINE CLEARING — MOVEMENT STEP (P. 94)
If not Pinned Down, Infantry or Mine-clearing Tank remove Minefield within 2"/5cm (after entering Minefield last turn). Cannot Move further, Shoot, Bombard, or Assault.

PASSENGERS (P. 34)
Dismount at the start or Mount at the end of Movement.
If not yet Moved, Transports can Move at Dash after Passengers mount.

TRANSPORTS (P. 35)
Send empty unarmoured or unarmed Transports to rear. May send other empty Transports to rear.
Bring forward Transports before Moving. Must be within 4"/10cm of Unit, and not within not within 4"/10cm of enemy, 16"/40cm if in Line of Sight unless Concealed.

SHOOTING

SHOOTING STEP (P. 38)
1. Check Range
2. Check Line of Sight
3. Check for Concealment
4. Declare Targets
5. Rotate to Face
6. Roll to Hit
7. Assign Hits
8. Roll Saves

WHICH WEAPONS CAN FIRE (P. 38)
Tanks or Aircraft may either fire all of its Machine-guns, or one other weapon.
Infantry or Guns may fire one weapon.
Cannot Shoot if Dash, Follow Me, or Cross Here.
Pinned Down Teams shoot as Moving

LINE OF SIGHT (P. 40)
Tall terrain blocks Line of Sight after 2"/5cm unless Range is 6"/15cm or less. Buildings and Hills block Line of Sight. Line of Sight to Aircraft is never blocked.
Smoke Screen blocks Line of Sight if Range is more than 6"/15cm.

CONCEALMENT (P. 41)
Concealed if entirely behind or in Tall or Short terrain, or at least half hidden by Buildings or Hills.
Stationary Infantry are Concealed.
Gun Teams in Foxholes are Concealed.

GONE TO GROUND (P. 44)
Teams that don't Move, Shoot, or Assault are Gone to Ground. Scouts can Move and still be Gone to Ground.

HOW MANY DICE (P. 44)
Roll one die per point of ROF. Halted ROF if did not Move and not Pinned Down, otherwise Moving ROF.

SCORE TO HIT (P. 44)
Roll Target Team's Is Hit On number:
Add +1 to score needed if:
- Range is over 16"/40cm
- Concealed (but not Gone to Ground)
- Shooter moved Out of Command
- Shooting through Smoke
- Shooting at Night

Add +2 to score needed if:
- Concealed and Gone to Ground

7+ OR MORE TO HIT (P. 44)
If need 7+, must roll 6 followed by 5+
If need 8+, must roll 6 followed by 6

©Battlefront Miniatures Ltd. 2019   Permission granted to photocopy for personal use only.   www.Team-Yankee.com